LOVE WISDOM MONEY

Praise for *Love Wisdom Money*

"Your book is a marvel—beautifully crafted, wonderful ideas, and a strain of you that glows through. I could feel as I read just how blessed your client families are and have been by your compassion and brilliance as you helped them unravel complex personal qualitative and quantitative issues and, as the sage said, made them simple. Yours is the art of the personne de confiance, one who carries the burdens for another, of absolute trust, of compassion for the human condition and love for human possibilities—yes the family fiduciary with a small f—fides—always faithful."

JAMES (JAY) E. HUGHES, JR., ESQ. is the author of the acclaimed classics *Family Wealth: Keeping It in the Family* and *Family: The Compact Among Generations*. He is also co-author with Susan Massenzio and Keith Whitaker of *The Cycle of the Gift: Family Wealth and Wisdom*, *The Voice of the Rising Generation*, and *Complete Family Wealth*, published by John Wiley & Sons.

"Forget dry financial advice. **Love Wisdom Money** *draws you in with compelling real-life family examples. Buddy Thomas illustrates the rich possibilities of generative wealth revealing the secrets to building a lasting legacy."*

JOHN "JOHN A" WARNICK is founder of the Purposeful Planning Institute, Fellow of the American College of Trust & Estate Counsel, and author of the *Purposeful Trust & Legacies Handbook*.

"It's a fantastic read. The stories are engaging and exemplify the key messages beautifully. I love the way you write! I also appreciate how you set the scene for each story with a location and date. As someone who has been "responsible" from birth, I appreciate the stewardship mindset. Love, wisdom, and money all weave together for readers (and me!) in a supportive, aspirational way. Bravo!"

CATHY CARROLL, President and Founder, Legacy Onward, and author of *Hug of War: How to Lead a Family Business with* both *Love* and *Logic*

"Love Wisdom Money is a must-read for families navigating the complexities of generational wealth. Buddy masterfully redefines what it means to be truly wealthy—not just in terms of money, but in relationships, wisdom, and stewardship. As an estate planning

attorney working with high-net-worth and ultra-high-net-worth individuals, I've seen firsthand how financial wealth alone is not enough to sustain a legacy. This book provides the essential framework for families to move beyond accumulation and into a purpose-driven approach to wealth."

DAVID YORK is an Attorney, Certified Public Accountant and Managing Partner with the Salt Lake City law firm of York Howell. He is the author of *The Gift of Lift: Harnessing the Power of Stewardship to Elevate the World* and co-author along with Andrew Howell of *Entrusted: Building a Legacy That Lasts* and *Riveted: 44 Values that Change the World.*

" ... offers a refreshing perspective that begins with a provocative question: "You're Rich. Now What?" This isn't just another financial planning book—it's a thoughtful exploration of wealth's purpose in our lives.

"The beauty of Thomas's approach lies in its wholeness.... This book serves as both roadmap and companion for those seeking to align their wealth with their most cherished values. Love Wisdom Money is that rare financial book that speaks to both head and heart."

PATTI BRENNAN, CFP, Key Financial, Inc., CEO, and Author, *Am I Going to Be Okay? (And is "Okay" Enough?)*

LOVE WISDOM MONEY

*The Family Fiduciary's
Guide to
Generative Wealth*

BUDDY THOMAS

Big Snowy
MEDIA

Love Wisdom Money: The Family Fiduciary's Guide to Generative Wealth

ISBN: 979-8-9896844-1-0

Published by: Big Snowy Media
©2025, Superplan Systems, LLC
All rights reserved.
Beyond Financial Security; Superior Planning Family Office; Love, Wisdom, Money; and Lifestyle, Portfolio, Legacy are trademarks of Superplan Systems, LLC.

Gameboards and Family Wealth Game are trademarks of Advice Engagement, Inc.

For information about special discounts for bulk purchases, please contact Big Snowy Media at: 209 E. Liberty Ave., Wheaton, IL 60187

Printed in the United States of America

*"No one can think that the weakening of the family ...
will prove beneficial to society as a whole.
The contrary is true: it poses a threat to the mature growth
of individuals, the cultivation of community values
and the moral progress of cities and countries."*

POPE FRANCIS

*To entrepreneurial families everywhere—whether you already
have more wealth than you need or are working toward
that goal—this book is for you.*

*It's also for those who deeply love their families, aspire to see them
thrive, and are committed to doing everything possible to position
them for success while embracing all that life has to offer.*

*And to you, trusted family wealth advisors, who understand
that family leaders rely on a network of professionals—accountants,
attorneys, wealth managers, investment bankers, and more—
to collaborate with and guide them in realizing their family's vision,
this book is for you as well.*

*Finally, to the dedicated specialists who stand by client families
as they navigate the complex challenges of building and sustaining
their legacies—your commitment makes a lasting impact,
and this book is written with your vital role in mind.*

Contents

Acknowledgements

This book would not exist without the inspiration, modeling, love, wisdom and support of many people, some of whom have gone before me:

First, my family: My wife, Liz, a gift from God the past forty years; our children, Dominic and George; and our daughter-in-law, Sam. Each has supported my passion for learning the essence of family wealth and communicating my findings to others;

My parents, Ann and Jim; and my brothers, Bob, Rich, Russ, and Terry, and their families. I am grateful for their unconditional love and creating a real-life model of a family wealth environment, which I have drawn upon through my profession and life's journey;

My grandparents and their families; and their ancestors. They passed on the timeless love, wisdom, and faith that is the foundation for all I know and hope to share;

The families we currently serve and their trusted advisors;

All the family fiduciaries, family members, and associates who took the risk to put their trust, confidence, family values, vision, and legacy in our firm's hands over the years. They had the courage to do what was in the best interest of those they love and serve regardless of the circumstances;

My mentors and colleagues;

Dan and Babs Sullivan and The Strategic Coach community, who planted the seeds of entrepreneurial clarity and confidence that helped me to deliver value and write books; Henry Whiffen who introduced me to the principles of integrated financial and estate planning; Scott Fithian who recognized the importance of family values over fiscal values; and Jay Hughes who brought clarity to the interdependencies of *Love Wisdom Money*;

Julie Dorosz, Shannon Mulvaney, and the community of the Purposeful Planning Institute for providing a fertile environment in which to discover and nurture the premise and ideas within this book and bring it to fruition;

John A Warnick, PPI Founder, a welcoming human being and friend, remarkable lawyer, and visionary leader with the uncanny ability to match people suited for collaboration, like the key people responsible for the creation of this book;

Laura Roser, who over the past ten years patiently helped me lay the foundation and find my voice;

Dave Goetz and Melissa Parks, cofounders, and Kirsten Tangeros, of Journey Sixty6, our editors and publishers, who professionally, graciously, and methodically drew out of me my most meaningful experiences and deepest sentiments in a way to make this book as engaging, educational, and entertaining as possible; and

Matthew and Brandy Coates, Founders, and Peter Wang, of Sweet Spot Media for their creative, energetic, strategic, awesome, digital and media, broadcast and communication efforts to get the word out about this book in the spirit of love and all that life has to offer.

Finally, to all members and associates of Superior Planning, past and present, who work together to deliver the nurturing environment and support to assist our client families in getting to where they want to go.

A Note from the Author

Cleveland, OH – Thanksgiving Day 1981

At 35, following a series of unexpected events, I left behind a decade-long dual career as an air traffic controller and the co-owner of two restaurants that ultimately failed.

Though my future felt uncertain that day, I was grateful for the incredible experiences I had gained. Still, I knew there was no going back. I found myself asking, *What could I possibly do next with such a checkered past?*

Despite the failure of the restaurants, I discovered that I genuinely enjoyed being an entrepreneur. Meanwhile, my time as an air traffic controller had been thrilling, challenging me to analyze data under pressure, remain calm and focused, and manage high-stakes complexity—skills that required quick, decisive action in a fast-paced environment.

With a bachelor's degree in psychology and economics, combined with the hard lessons from my restaurant failures, I felt I had earned a school-of-hard-knocks master's degree in how not to be an entrepreneur.

Within a few months, I discovered this odd variety of skills translated seamlessly into the relatively new world of financial planning. Just as I guided planes safely through turbulent and crowded skies and delivered dining experiences customized for family life events (weddings, baptisms, birthday parties, graduations, retirements, and funerals), it was natural for me to help family leaders navigate the complexities of their family life dynamics and family financial situations.

This journey led to the founding of Superior Planning,^{SM} a firm dedicated to supporting and guiding family leaders as they work toward their ideal vision of family wealth. What started as a career choice gradually became a passion as I realized I could not only assist families with immediate financial planning but also help those striving to make a transformational impact in their lives and the lives of their loved ones.

Since that late November day so many years ago, I've had the privilege of working with hundreds of family leaders. Together, we've enriched their lifestyles, built and protected their portfolios, and created distinctive legacies. I've witnessed firsthand the positive impact of their efforts—not just on themselves and their families, but also on the businesses they lead and the communities they serve.

Somewhere along the way, my work evolved from a career into my life's purpose—my personal and professional reason for being. It's work I love, work I'm committed to doing with excellence, and work I feel compelled to continuously improve upon for as long as I can.

For that blessing, I am, and always will be, profoundly grateful.

WHY THIS BOOK NOW?

The world has been in a constant state of flux since I began this journey, and that change seems to be accelerating with no end in sight. When it comes to family wealth, we've witnessed significant changes: greater financial abundance, shifting lifestyle behaviors, rapid technological advancements, an expanded universe of investment options, elevated standards of living, and increasingly broad expectations for estate planning and desired outcomes.

The landscape of financial advising has also shifted significantly. Today, deeper levels of due diligence and compliance are not just recommended—they're essential for success. This growing complexity demands fresh perspectives, innovative approaches, and strong interpersonal relationships. Over the years, we've witnessed tremendous successes as well as difficult failures—families who thrive and grow, and others who, despite their best intentions, struggle to hold on.

This book draws on my personal experiences and those of my clients, offering insights and guidelines to help you, the family leader, and you, the trusted advisor, work together to overcome obstacles, seize opportunities, and pave the way for future generations.

Grounded in love, wisdom, and financial stewardship, this book is not a road map but a treasure map—one only you, the family leader, can draw, because only you know where you want to go. Its purpose is to help you navigate the complexities of family wealth, so you can enjoy an abundant life and prepare your loved ones to continue the journey after you.

To that end, I am at your service and wish you the very best life has to offer.

Sincerely,

Buddy Thomas
Thanksgiving Day 2024

YOU'RE RICH. NOW WHAT?

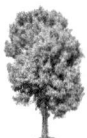

"Money, it's a gas. Grab that cash with both hands and make a stash."

PINK FLOYD

Never lose sight of the big picture, especially when it comes to generational wealth.

If you are reading this book, you either have or intend to have generational wealth, which can be defined as "any kind of assets that are passed down from one generation to the next." It's the kind of wealth most people consider their legacy.

But there is another kind of wealth—generative wealth—a concept rarely discussed until now because it has often seemed out of reach. Generative wealth represents an entirely different dimension of wealth: the kind that creates and sustains itself.

When we think of wealth, we conventionally think of assets and money. I am here to tell you, there is far more to family wealth than money. But let's start there anyway.

Del Mar, CA – January 21, 1999

Our prospective clients were euphoric. The couple had just sold their small tech company to the major conglomerate Sprint for somewhere in the vicinity of $8 million.[A] It was paid to them mostly in Sprint company stock, which rapidly appreciated. Within months, on the cusp of the dot-com boom, the value of their stock had skyrocketed by 50% to over $12 million.[B]

They asked, "What do we do now that we are financially independent?"

After getting to know them a bit better, I asked, "What do you want the money to do for you?"

They responded almost in unison: "Take care of our family for life."

The entrepreneurial family business leader's spouse went on to say with a smile, "And one more thing. I would like to buy the biggest private jet one can fly alone. I already have a smaller one and have my eye on the newest model that just came out." Not having yet cashed in on their windfall, he explained that they were subsidizing the cost of their current plane by chartering it out from time to time.

Their goals were simple: a secure lifestyle and a bigger plane.

After a few more meetings we had a plan. By this time, the value of their stock had continued to rise and was up over 400% from when they got it, now unbelievably at a market price of

---

[A] In 1999, $8 million had purchasing power of approximately $15.3 million in 2024. These numbers were determined by using an inflation calculator. For example, see "CPI Inflation Calculator," U.S. Bureau of Labor Statistics, https://www.bls.gov/data/inflation_calculator.htm.

[B] In 1999, $12 million had purchasing power of approximately $23 million in 2024.

[C] In 1999, $35 million had purchasing power of approximately $67 million in 2024.

over \$35 million.[C]

The initial plan was also simple: Contribute an initial \$10 million of appreciated stock to a tax advantaged trust designed to generate \$500,000 per year income for life. At the time, it was more than enough to both provide a lifestyle income and finance the plane. If they wanted more lifetime income they could add more stock to the trust later.

When we discussed the future beyond today's concerns and goals, they raised additional questions about protecting, investing, and managing the \$25 million portfolio balance, the potential impact of their newfound wealth on their children, and strategies to minimize or prepare for their new estate tax liability. Unfortunately, we never had a chance to explore or act on anything further.

When we think of wealth, we conventionally think of assets and money. There is far more to family wealth than money.

Almost every planning failure I have experienced has been due to one major human condition: People are often unwilling to do what they need to do to get what they say they want.

There is something psychological about inaction. Call it fear, greed, procrastination, resistance to change, whatever. Such was the case with this couple. They could not execute. The price of their stock continued to rise. With the market value over \$40 million,[D] I said, "Great, we have \$5 million more than we did last week. How would you like to proceed?" I was astounded by their answer.

[D] In 1999, \$40 million had purchasing power of approximately \$76.8 million in 2024.

"Analysts are projecting the stock to double again soon, so we have decided to wait and see," they said.

I said, "All of it?"

Despite my efforts and those of all their other advisors, nothing could sway their decision. As the saying goes, "You can lead a horse to water …"

Within a week, it climbed by yet another $5 million. Still no change of heart. Then the share price began to flutter. Then drop. Slowly at first, then like a rock. We touched base a few times on the way down, but they were sure it would rebound and chose to wait it out. The NAS-DAQ market index, on which their stock was listed, rose fivefold between 1995 and 2000, then saw an almost 77% drop, resulting in a loss of billions of dollars. It took almost 15 years for that entire market to recover.[1]

Plan, execute, monitor the results, adapt accordingly. Repeat.

Though we continued to reach out to them during the downturn, we eventually lost contact. At that time, the estimated value of the stock was less than half of the original sale price of the business (an approximately $40 million paper loss from its peak value).

We hadn't seen each other for a few years, and when we finally reconnected, they said, "We're sorry we didn't return your calls. We felt there was really nothing to talk about." I asked how they were doing. They said, "We're OK. Nothing much changed. The family is fine, and we still enjoy using the plane and chartering it out." I had never seen—and still have not seen—such a catastrophic, self-inflicted missed opportunity.

Planning is only the beginning. When opportunity knocks— and not really that hard—it is important to answer. Plan, execute, monitor the results, adapt accordingly. Repeat.

Palos Verdes, CA – November 2, 2000

In a serendipitous turn of events, we were introduced to another couple who had sold their tech company in 1999 for $8 million. Theirs was an all-cash deal, and despite being savvy market investors, by the end of that crazy year 2000, their $8 million had turned to $7 million. Not that bad for the times.

Introduced to our firm by one of their trusted advisors, we quickly established a strong rapport. In our first meeting, the founder's engineering background led them to inquire about our process. After we briefly described the benefits of our Lifestyle, Portfolio, and Legacy system, and through the strength of their relationship with the referrer, they engaged our firm on the spot.

Early on in our engagement, we asked the same question of them that we asked the previous couple: "What do you want your money to do for you?" We got a similar response. They wanted to take care of their family for life, except there was no airplane this time. (Though they did want to dispose of the boat they hadn't been using.)

Their financial situation was a bit different than the other couple's. Instead of a single rapidly appreciating stock, they had a diversified portfolio of mostly individual stocks, which they were comfortable with despite their recent market performance. Like the other couple, they were also concerned about how their newfound wealth would affect their children and were looking for strategies to mitigate their estate tax liability.

As process-oriented and as thorough as they were, it took the better part of the year to finalize their investment policy statement and design a portfolio that aligned with their needs along with a tax reduction strategy developed in collaboration with their CPA. By August 2001, they were ready to implement the plan. In early September, the paperwork was sent to electronically execute the SELL trade orders, liquidating the holdings that didn't align with their new asset allocation. Wire transfers were also authorized to BUY the new investments once the proceeds were available. The execution was flawless. What could possibly go wrong?

For this family, whose money was literally unreach-able, the four days of halted market activity were agonizing.

Most of the money was "on the wire," or as someone put it "in cyberspace," at the time of the 9/11 attacks. Suddenly, all the markets and banks closed, freezing all transactions. No one knew what happened or what would happen next. All we could do was watch, wait, and grieve for the lives lost, the property destroyed, and the profound impact the terrorist attacks had on our country.

For this family, whose money was literally unreachable, the four days of halted market activity were agonizing. They even wondered, *Will we ever see that money again?* However, thanks to the stability of our economic system, all securities trades were made and it all arrived intact. This harrowing experience was not self-imposed. They did everything humanly possible to act in the best interest of their family. Yet, they were still at the whim of life events.

In both cases, blind luck played a major role in the outcome. The first family had extremely good luck they let slip away before it turned bad; and the second had no control over extremely bad luck that eventually turned out to benefit them as they unconsciously sold high and bought low.

Feeling lucky is not a dependable investment strategy. However, over the years of being planners we have learned luck should never be ignored. It's critical to keep in mind that good luck or bad luck could befall anyone at any time. The key is to be prepared to mitigate its adverse effects when it works against you and take advantage of it when it is in your favor.

WHERE ARE YOU ON YOUR FAMILY WEALTH JOURNEY?

A marketing consultant once asked me to describe the "personas" of the families we serve. Through research, we identified five distinct categories, each corresponding to a phase on what we now call the family wealth continuum.

One common thread among our clients was that they were nearly all entrepreneurial business owners who valued both family and business. Surprisingly, their financial growth stemmed from a wide range of industries, with no more than two families in the same sector.

We also observed that the families fell into one of five phases along their intergenerational wealth journey: Accumulators, Harvesters, Stewards, Survivors, or Heirs. Each category reflected a specific stage in their family's life cycle and approach to managing wealth.

FAMILY WEALTH CONTINUUM

Looking at our client base from this perspective, we realized some families had gone through this family wealth continuum cycle for multiple generations, each one building on the one before. The graphic above, starting at the bottom—or six o'clock position—shows a progressive clockwise journey.

Most young families start out as Accumulators, focused on building their wealth and achieving financial independence. For example, the Del Mar couple had just sold their tech company for $8 million and rapidly saw their stock portfolio skyrocket to over $40 million during the dot-com boom. Their story highlights the potential of the Accumulator phase, but also the risks of inaction. Despite having a clear desire to secure their family's future, they hesitated to execute their plan, ultimately missing the opportunity to preserve their wealth before the market turned.

Families that succeed as Accumulators often transition into Harvesters, enjoying the fruits of their labor by living off what they've built. This is where the vast majority of people are content to remain. However, a small percentage of families develop a different mindset and evolve into Stewards—those who focus on nurturing and preserving their family wealth for themselves and future generations.

For example, the Palos Verdes couple approached their new-found wealth with a process-oriented approach. Unlike the Del Mar family, they executed their plan and diversified their portfolio to mitigate risks, even amid the uncertainties following the 9/11 attacks. This Stewardship mindset not only secured their financial stability but also laid the groundwork for their children to inherit a carefully managed legacy.

Families who embrace Stewardship often take proactive steps to educate their Heirs.

When the first spouse passes, the Survivor takes the reins to finalize the estate plan and ensure the wealth is positioned for the next generation. Survivors play a crucial role in preparing the family wealth for the Heirs, who will inherit the responsibility of continuing the cycle, often beginning again as Accumulators.

Our research also showed that families who embrace Stewardship usually take proactive steps to educate their Heirs, preparing them for the possibility of achieving generational or even generative family wealth.

BEYOND FINANCIAL SECURITY

The balance of this book explores the possibilities that lie ahead for your family. It focuses on how you can uniquely nurture and enrich your family wealth—your love, wisdom, and money—to a place beyond financial security based on your unique values, vision, and goals. Additionally, if you choose (and I encourage you to do so), you can receive guidance in these pages on positioning your family members and trusted advisors to continue this process for future generations. Chapters one through five lay the philosophical framework, helping you define your family's values, explore the role of love and wisdom in wealth, and understand the psychological and relational dynamics that shape financial decision-making. Chapters six through ten shift to practical application, guiding you through essential financial strategies—including cash flow management, portfolio design, estate planning, and the role of a modern family office—to ensure your wealth serves both present and future generations.

I share insights from working directly with hundreds of entrepreneurial families on their journeys—how they achieved success, faced failures, navigated challenges, and implemented strategies that worked (or didn't). You'll also discover valuable methods to protect and grow your family wealth—your love, wisdom, and money.

To paraphrase Dan Sullivan, one of the world's leading entrepreneurial coaches: When your life expectancy is shorter than the time you've already lived, the only way to make your future bigger than your past is by focusing on something beyond yourself.[2]

If all this sounds interesting, I have a couple of questions for you …

1

WHO ARE YOU? WHAT DO YOU WANT?

"If you get to my age in life and nobody thinks well of you, I don't care how big your bank account is, your life is a disaster."

WARREN BUFFET

La Costa, CA – November 18, 2009

How much money did you make last year?"

"I don't know," my prospective client said. "Two, three million maybe?"

His response surprised me, not so much because he didn't really know how much his business pulled in the previous year, but because I had seen the business income that he had reported on a draft of his tax return—$300,000.

"So, your business made between $2 million and $3 million, but you reported only $300,000 on your tax return?"

"It's a tax return," he answered, as if pointing out the obvious. "No one puts the real number on their tax return. Everyone lies. Besides, I'm rich now and rich people don't pay taxes."

I called his accountant. "Where did you get that number?"

"That's the number he gave me. It's about the same as it has been for years."

This blew me away. "You didn't verify it? Look into it?"

"Not my job," his accountant said. "I just do taxes."

Prior to that, the prospect had engaged in one business venture after another, getting by on nominal profits with the habit of underreporting low six-figure incomes. Until suddenly he stumbled on a product that people snatched off the shelves.

Then the business started to scale, and the money flowed in, but he continued to operate from his old scarcity mentality paradigm: Everybody lies, and rich people don't pay taxes.

The money also flowed out. One luxury car after another. Then a new home in an upscale neighborhood. He became the quintessential consumer, with an all-too-easy rhythm of making and spending. And with no thought of the effects of taxation.

We were reluctant about taking on this entrepreneur as a client. Though his actions were misdirected, we felt his heart was in the right place, and he genuinely wanted to do the right thing. So, we engaged him with the contingency that he would establish a formalized accounting process and file legitimate tax returns, something he surprisingly seemed to embrace enthusiastically. We helped him find a new accountant who also cautiously saw the promise in setting this entrepreneur straight. Or so we thought.

When the client first saw the updated tax returns and how

much he owed, he asked his new CPA, "Whose side are you on?"

The accountant replied, "Yours! If you don't pay what you owe, the IRS and the state of California will come to your house."

A hard pill to swallow for someone who had never done it before, but the client agreed. He filed the proper returns and made his first payments. However, as subsequent estimated payments came due, there seemed to always be something else that called for the money. Time passed, and his old habits prevailed. We parted ways. You might guess what came next. He got in arrears on his payments, wrongfully believing, "The tax collectors will wait!" Eventually, the Feds came for him.

> *Even love and money are not enough without the integrity, prudence, and stabilizing force of wisdom.*

He wasn't there when the agents arrived, but his wife was. Blindsided, she confronted him in their bedroom when he got home.

"It'll be fine," he said, and of course it wasn't. Penalties, interest, competition, and mismanagement eventually prevailed. This situation is a classic example of how even love and money are not enough without the integrity, prudence, and stabilizing force of wisdom.

THE RISE OF THE FAMILY FIDUCIARY

The tragedy of this story is that it could have been avoided. The client had all he needed available to him: a loving family, a successful business, and trustworthy, competent advisors. But he lost it all because of one thing: a reluctance to grow beyond his consumer mentality.

He focused solely on the immediate gratification that money could buy, overlooking the responsibilities and opportunities that come with wealth. He failed to recognize that wealth demands principled values, a potentially grander vision, responsibilities, and opportunities beyond mere consumption. He was a family leader, but the values on which he was making decisions about his family wealth were flawed. He lacked both the understanding and integrity necessary to build his family wealth in a way that would endure and enrich his family. He did not hold himself to the higher standard of "family fiduciary," one who lives up to both their legal responsibility for the property entrusted to them and their moral responsibility of putting the best interests of others above their own.

> **Wealth demands principled values, a potentially grander vision, responsibilities, and opportunities beyond mere consumption.**

Someone once asked me, "What if it's not about you?" That question shifted my perspective and helped me understand the mindset of a family fiduciary as a steward. For a steward, serving a larger purpose—something greater than themselves—is central to their worldview. The individual self is no longer the center of the universe; their responsibility to others is.

THE FAMILY FIDUCIARY STEWARD MINDSET

In *The Gift of Lift: Harnessing the Power of Stewardship to Elevate the World*, David York, a world-class estate planning attorney, explores an XY graph framework for understanding four different categories of fiduciary stewardship and responsibility.[1]

He uses two key dimensions to measure individual psychological priorities: the X-axis (horizontal plane) measures one's willingness to exert effort toward a goal, while the Y-axis (vertical plane) measures concern for others. The X-axis ranges from minimal effort to full commitment. The Y-axis ranges from self-centered to highly altruistic. Based on these dimensions, York identifies four distinct categories of individual tendencies, determined by their position within the four quadrants of the graph.

- **Consumers** (lower left quadrant) primarily focus on themselves with little interest in working (low altruism, low effort).
- **Dreamers** (upper left quadrant) care about others and may have grand visions, but don't do much about it (high altruism, low effort).
- **Owners** (lower right quadrant) tend to be self-focused but willing to do what's necessary for their own benefit (low altruism, high effort).
- **Stewards** (upper right quadrant) balance their concern for others with a strong commitment to working to benefit both themselves and those around them (high altruism, high effort).

The former "tax averse" client, mentioned earlier in this chapter, was more a consumer than anything else, primarily focused on a lifestyle of spending. When his fourth car, a Ferrari, broke down, he simply bought another—a Lamborghini.

The irony was, his life of consumption in the lower left quadrant, with little other counterbalancing priorities to center or anchor him, ultimately consumed him ... and his family.

In contrast, the stewardship life in the upper right quadrant sets the stage for an ever increasing, albeit measured, level of growth and success. Growth and success, whatever they may be and however they are attained, always leave something missing and something more to be done.

The stewardship life in the upper right quadrant sets the stage for an ever increasing level of growth and success.

While we all exhibit traits from each of the four quadrants, I've observed that family fiduciary stewards who embrace their legal and moral responsibilities with enthusiasm—one step at a time, one day at a time—have the most natural path to fostering both personal and family wealth growth.

Now let's turn the lens inward. Here's a quick self-evaluation: Where on the graph do you fall? How do you feel about where you are? And what, if anything, would you want to do about it?

AN INTERNAL GUIDANCE SYSTEM

From wherever you are on the grid personally, your position of family fiduciary steward demands some kind of guidance system that operates like a gyroscope: a mindset to counterbalance the three dimensions of family wealth—love, wisdom, and money. This "gyroscope mindset" will enable you to do what you can to keep your family on course and increase the chances of getting you all where you want to go. As your family's fiduciary steward, you are ultimately responsible for shepherding your family's resources, keeping your best interest and theirs in mind, and making family wealth protection and growth decisions that will have significant implications.

There are plenty of larger-than-life examples of wildly successful entrepreneurs who have made decisions based on their values, for the whole world to see. Elon Musk has a cosmic vision for saving humanity; his family at the time of this writing—numerous children with numerous wives—illustrates an aspect of his individual preference family values.

Your life is no different. The decisions you make based on what you value and what you envision will be a manifestation of those values and eventually transform into your legacy. We are all building our legacies each day, with every decision we make, all being a direct result of who we are (what we value) and what we want (the future we have in mind).

Beaver Creek, CO – February 29, 2024

I was invited to address seventeen entrepreneurial real estate developers and business owners at their annual mastermind retreat. As family leaders, they were interested in knowing more about the inner workings of family offices and how such organizations might benefit them both personally and in their businesses. Prior to diving into the inner workings of family office operations, benefits, opportunities, and pitfalls, I hoped to reframe their relationship with their family wealth in a way that might positively enhance the development of their own values, visions, and goals. In their thirties and early forties, these men and women were primarily focused on creating and accumulating financial wealth.

I had a wacky idea, and unsure how it would land with my audience, I took a chance.

"Take out your phone," I said as I began. "I would like you to take a selfie. Take a couple of shots so you get a good one. This is for your family, to show them how much you love them and how happy they make you—so you can share it with them later."

I didn't have to ask twice. They lit up and began to pose for their selfies. It was amazing how they jumped into character as their family's patriarchs and matriarchs—even at their youthful ages. Apparently, they were happy with the outcomes as they began to share the results smiling with each other.

Then I said, "Pick your favorite picture of yourself, the one you think your family will like the most and look at it. I would now like to introduce you to someone: Please meet your family fiduciary. The person responsible for your family wealth. The person most responsible for what happens to your family's love, wisdom, and money today and very likely for years and even decades to come."

Suddenly, everyone got a bit more serious. I wanted to impress upon these highly energetic, driven entrepreneurs that they as leaders of their families have a responsibility that is much grander than merely accumulating more and growing their financial portfolios. I was hoping they could see, it's not just about them and the money. Based on their attention to and interest in the presentation I gave that morning, it was clear they grasped a broader and deeper understanding of the significance of their roles in their families at a whole new level. As their family fiduciaries, they were beginning to see themselves as the stewards of their three-dimensional family wealth.

That doesn't mean we didn't talk a lot about money that day. Making money is still a primary goal. It's as important as ever, yet in a much broader context. Money is the currency by which we afford our security and liberty, finance our dreams, and keep score. Money, when balanced with fiduciary stewardship, unconditional love, and generations of hard-earned wisdom, can transform into integrated family wealth.

Money, when balanced with fiduciary stewardship, unconditional love, and generations of hard-earned wisdom, can transform into integrated family wealth.

This kind of wealth supports and nurtures future generations, allowing them to depend on it, learn from it, and prosper in their own ways. It introduces an expanded role for wealth creators and inheritors, emphasizing the responsibility of managing the full spectrum of family wealth.

This chapter reframes conventional wisdom about wealth management, defining the family fiduciary as a steward of three-dimensional family wealth: financial assets, intellectual property, and family values. By embracing this role, you can sustain and grow your financial resources, enrich your family's shared values and love, and contribute to making the world a better place.

By now, I hope you have a clearer understanding of the questions that opened this chapter: *Who are you?* and *What do you want?*—particularly when it comes to nurturing and growing your family wealth.

In the next three chapters, we will explore the three dimensions of family wealth—love, wisdom, and money—examining how they relate to and integrate with one another. You'll also learn how to create your own family wealth gyroscope, a tool to balance these dynamics and keep you on course toward realizing your vision for your family's future.

Now, let's talk about love.

2

WHAT'S LOVE GOT TO DO WITH IT?

"Wealth, my son, should never be your goal in life. Your words are eloquent but they are mere words. True wealth is of the heart, not of the purse."

OG MANDINO

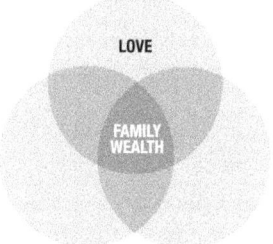

THREE DIMENSIONS

LOVE

FAMILY WEALTH

San Diego, CA – May 25, 2008

Two of my wife's and my longtime friends, like us, built their family through adoption. They devotedly raised three daughters. The youngest, barely in her teens, struggled with mental illness; it was a chaotic convergence of puberty, a bipolar condition, and self-medicating with a combination of prescription and street drugs. It led her to ongoing psychotherapeutic outpatient treatment. With mental illness, there are never quick fixes. We wish there were three easy steps or a straight path to recovery and wholeness. But there aren't.

Early one Sunday morning, the mother woke up first and went to the kitchen to make coffee. As her husband lay in bed, he heard a sharp scream. When he looked into the kitchen, he saw his bloodied wife lying on the floor and his troubled daughter holding a hammer. His daughter had bludgeoned her mother to death. A confrontation with his daughter ensued until her body went limp and she fell silent, and she was eventually subdued enough to be turned over to the authorities.

At the mother's funeral about a week later, no one in attendance could believe or understand what had happened. His face grief-stricken, the father stood up and slowly walked to the pulpit to give his wife's eulogy. She was a kind, caring, and giving person—loved by all who knew her. She was a teacher, devoted spouse, attentive mother, and community volunteer armed with a positive, get-things-done disposition. This was a tremendous loss for all of us who loved her, but especially for her husband and children.

As our friend closed the eulogy, he looked up at all those in attendance and said to his daughter, who was incarcerated and unable to attend, "I forgive you, and I will always love you."

Writing this all these years later, I still struggle to absorb the magnitude of his love and compassion. How could he forgive the person responsible for his wife's demise? How could he offer gracious compassion to the perpetrator when the woman he loved, who meant so much to him and his family, was gone? His absolution, however, was not mere lip service. Nor was it a heroic statement fabricated in the fog of tragedy. He meant it in his heart and financed every penny of her legal defense even though she may spend the rest of her life in prison. To this day, he is her biggest advocate.

It's a horrific story, hard to recount and hard to read, I'm sure. But it is a living manifestation of the nature of unconditional love. "Unconditional" means no strings attached. No matter how terrible a person's actions, nothing can stop love from being expressed. Authentic forgiveness as demonstrated here may perhaps be among the greatest expressions there are of unconditional love.

A few years later, the father remarried a woman whose first marriage had also ended in tragedy. At their wedding dinner, they gave small Japanese kintsugi bowls as gifts to those attending. Kintsugi is the ancient art of putting broken pieces of pottery back together with gold, where the melded pottery is structurally stronger than if it were made entirely of the original material. This newly married, vibrant couple now spends much of their time as grief counselors, helping others faced with tragic circumstances find their way on the dark journey back from heartbreaking loss.

"Unconditional" means no strings attached.

Most of us believe we love unconditionally. Believing, though, is easy. The act of loving unconditionally is not. Or is it? We only know whether our love is truly unconditional when it's tested.

And that test can be unthinkable. But that tested love is the natural generative force from which the entire family loves, grows, and prospers today and into the future. Without love, family wealth cannot exist.

Previously I likened the role of the family fiduciary to that of a gyroscope, counterbalancing the three dimensions of family wealth: love, wisdom, and money. Financial wealth alone is frequently fleeting, often consumed in one's lifetime or, even if significant, within a generation or two. But as we have seen, family wealth anchored in love has the potential to endure indefinitely despite the insurmountable obstacles that families are called upon to face.

> *Family wealth anchored in love has the potential to endure indefinitely despite the insurmountable obstacles that families are called upon to face.*

FOUNDATIONAL LOVE

In his book *The Four Loves*, mid-20th century British author and intellectual C.S. Lewis wrote about the nature of love in its many forms.[1] He identified four basic types of love, experienced between people as it grows: friendship, affection, eros (romantic), and ultimately charity (the love of community, each other). All four forms of love find expression in the family and are essential building blocks that establish the foundation of family wealth.

Friends are the people you choose to spend time and work with, and the people you trust alongside you to encounter life's events. For many families, this includes a variety of trusted advisors and employees who, over time, can be known to put your needs ahead of their own. Often these relationships move from being merely professional to deep, long-lasting friendships.

Affection grows beyond friendship and is most naturally shared more among family members and other extremely close personal and business relationships. As you will see in a later chapter, it is this affinity that my brothers and I have for each other that helped us power through the intergenerational transition of my father's company.

INTIMATE LOVE

Eros is, well, the basic human instinct that often leads to the next generation of family members. Eros is an intensifying force, singular in its focus on one person, with whom you share a union built on passion, fire, and mutual respect. It is within the conflux of this desire and unity that life is conceived and regenerated. Eros ebbs and flows in intensity—and can be initiated, carried along, strengthened and even intensified by the more basic currents of friendship and affection.

Like affection but much more invigorating, eros is connected to biology and an inborn drive inside each of us for physical and spiritual bonding with another human being, yet in the most intimate way possible. True romance, not to be confused with simply physical lust, is like an affectionate friendship on steroids. These initial emotions can lead to the creation of families and even more love. Civilized humanity itself would likely cease without it.

Unlike other types of love, the endearing, authentic, and romantic nature of eros can be somewhat confusing. Perhaps due to self-limiting human reasoning, it often seems the most difficult to attain. Genuine romance demands the authentic union of the physical, emotional, and spiritual. In an enduring marriage, eros is the love for the spouse you depend on today and age with until the end. Though the fires of your passion may quiet, the embers linger.

ULTIMATE LOVE

According to Lewis, these three loves are drawn up into the fourth love, the greatest and most noble love of all. Charity, the love of community.

Charity originates with God (or however you describe the invisible, benevolent force in the universe outside you) and is poured into us. This is the love that is essential for your family, and the family of humanity for that matter, to be sustained and continue to grow and evolve into the future. This is the root and combination of all love that the family fiduciary steward embraces as the ultimate driving force of true family wealth.

We do not generate charity; we simply allow it to flow through us to others, underscoring its supernatural unconditional nature. This kind of love is not action, but the source of action. It is the life-giving source of love that flows from you into the world when you let it. If friendship is betrayed, the sweetness of your affection can turn bitter; the passionate fire of eros can die down and evaporate over time. However, charitable unconditional love continues to flow from its universal unlimited source, as the deep-rooted goodness that makes us human.

And, whether we feel it or allow it to manifest itself, it persists and endures.

Ultimately, forgiveness, such as that of our friend who lost his wife at the hands of his daughter, can only be the work of charity. This love is the release—letting go—of the deep wrong inflicted upon us. When allowed to be unconditional, charity prevails through all challenges to ensure that the family carries on. According to St. Paul, love bears, believes, hopes, and endures all things.[2]

Just as we see unconditional love guiding difficult decisions like offering forgiveness, we also see it expressed in the everyday sacrifices that family members make to ensure the well-being of their loved ones. Love in action is the essence of family wealth and its very foundation.

[Charity] is the root and combination of all love that the family fiduciary steward embraces as the ultimate driving force of true family wealth.

Without love, there can be no family. With it, a family is empowered to be what it was meant to be. True love will help a family find and keep its true north, that orienting, fixed point in a world that continues to change at a dizzying pace. While true love resists definition, you know it when you see it. It is observed and measured in the action it initiates.

To love someone is to sacrifice, listen, empathize, appreciate, and affirm them. True love is not ownership but its opposite. It is giving—and serving. Charity engages in the work of love for the sake of others, not yourself.

NUCLEAR ENERGY

While these different forms of love—friendship, affection, eros, and charity—are vital to nurturing family wealth, the structure and openness of the family unit also plays a crucial role in determining whether this wealth can endure and thrive across generations. The term "nuclear family," coined in the 20th century, originally described the primary family unit as a married couple with children. While somewhat outdated, the phrase has since evolved to encompass a wide variety of family configurations, each capable of embodying the same—if not greater—integrity of family wealth as defined in the original concept.

In his groundbreaking book *Family: The Compact Among Generations*, James Hughes uses the phrase "families of affinity" to describe the kinds of financially wealthy families most likely to persist in subsequent generations. He makes the distinction between families who define themselves by blood and genetic lineage alone, and families of affinity who are open to promoting family with the inclusion of new family members.

Love in action is the essence of family wealth and its very foundation.

He suggests that "families of blood" close their systems to new members outside the genetic lineage, thereby missing out on the energy, talents, and perspectives these individuals might bring. In contrast, Hughes describes families of affinity as those that remain open, welcoming new members through birth, adoption, marriage, or mutual attraction—creating a dynamic system that fosters growth and helps the family flourish.

Insular families that "create out-laws out of their in-laws perform less well," Hughes says. Affinity families, by contrast, grow through "fusion." Hughes compares family members to sources of energy—each bringing their positive affection to create a powerful, unified force. This collective energy not only enhances the lives of each individual but also strengthens the family's bond and positively impacts the world around them.

Families of affinity do not form by chance. Every family I have worked with that embodies the principles of a family of affinity has done so with intention. They understand what they treasure and dedicate themselves to nurturing and growing it. They pour their hearts into this effort, becoming love in action—outward expressions of unconditional love. It is love without limits, expanding the nuclear family to grow its circle of influence and impact rather than restricting it.

Unconditional love always seeks to contribute to the life of the family as it expands. As Hughes says, "Families of affinity, not families of blood, will be those who flourish five generations into the future, and can imagine going on from there in an unending upward spiral of new flourishing generations."[3] In the words of Stephen Covey, "My friend, love is a verb. Love— the feeling—is a fruit of love, the verb."[4] In other words the feeling derives from the action and is not the reason for it. It's the action—the intention, commitment, and follow through—that gives love its generative power, especially when it's tested.

THE EXTRAORDINARY POWER OF LOVE IN ACTION

So far, we have laid the groundwork for understanding the fundamental force that initiates and enriches family wealth: the transformative power of love.

Unlike commercial enterprises, a family enterprise— the combined operation of your family's love, wisdom, and financial wealth—is uniquely shaped by the love your family members have for one another. Recognizing this distinction elevates your enterprising family above that of any commercial, bureaucratic, or even philanthropic enterprise. In contrast to nonfamily organizations, family wealth rooted in love, appreciated and nurtured, can be sustained for many generations, even during times of restricted, meager, or ordinary economic circumstances. However, as powerful as it is, the growth of family wealth never just happens, nor can it be sustained by love alone.

Families of affinity do not form by chance.

There is another, almost as powerful and every bit as essential, elemental force of nature necessary for healthy family wealth. In a word: wisdom.

3

HEALTHY, WEALTHY, AND WISE

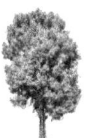

"Wisdom is to be sensitive to this situation, to this person. ... If the heart is unobstructed, the result is love."

ANTHONY DE MELLO

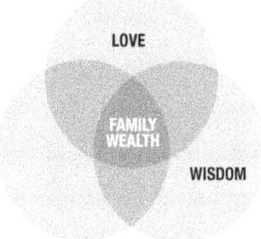

THREE DIMENSIONS

LOVE

FAMILY WEALTH

WISDOM

Unconditional love defies logic and reason, offering something far deeper. But love is more than a powerful force of nature that draws people together—it's also what sustains them.

With love comes a natural commitment to others. Commitment brings an all-in responsibility. That responsibility leaves no room for turning back, leading to moments of trial and error. And as we know, trial and error is one of life's greatest teachers, offering invaluable wisdom along the way.

Where genuine unconditional love is, wisdom will surely follow.

NOT SO PRACTICAL CONVENTIONAL WISDOM

John Kenneth Galbraith introduced the concept of modern societal accumulated wisdom, or "conventional wisdom," in his highly regarded 1958 book *The Affluent Society*. He described the intellectual and economic status of industrialized society at the turn of the 20th century.

By conventional wisdom, Galbraith referred to the generally accepted beliefs and ideas prevalent in society, especially within the context of economics, public policy, and social behavior. He argued that these widely held beliefs are often not questioned or critically examined, even when they may no longer serve the public interest.

Galbraith was specifically critical of the way economic policies and societal attitudes during the mid-20th century were shaped by outdated notions of wealth, progress, and security, which were rooted in earlier agrarian and industrial age eras. He believed that society's reliance on these outdated ideas hindered necessary change and innovation. He pointed out that conventional wisdom tends to resist change because when an idea is unfamiliar it threatens the illusion of comfort and the stability of the status quo even when it may no longer be relevant or accurate.

Galbraith also argued that the traditional dilemma faced by the working man—choosing between the security of guaranteed employment and the potential for greater earnings as a risk-taking entrepreneur—was a false choice. He posited that these two options were not mutually exclusive but could, in fact, work together as synergistic forces.[1] This balance would empower working families to pursue both security and entrepreneurial opportunities without having to choose one over the other.

For many, this was and may still be an elusive view of wisdom.

While Galbraith critiqued the dangers of relying on outdated conventional wisdom in relation to macroeconomic trends, his insights can also be applied to managing family wealth. Given that the individual and collective intellectual and experiential well-being of each family member is at stake, family wisdom—

Love is more than a powerful force of nature that draws people together—it's also what sustains them.

like societal wisdom—must continuously evolve to address the ever-changing circumstances, challenges, and opportunities the family faces at an increasing pace.

We all spring from the merger of two families that literally and figuratively lay the groundwork and shape who we become. Dual histories that comingle and synergize. In this we are alike, though everything else about us may be different.

Bugnara, Italy – February 18, 1910

My paternal grandparents, Dominic and Paula, were born and

spent their early years in a valley in Central Italy. They married during difficult economic times, when local employment opportunities were scarce. Drawn by the possibilities America offered at the turn of the 20th century, they decided to emigrate and seek a better future.

Sponsored by relatives, they relocated to the burgeoning industrialized steel mill cities of northeastern Ohio. A product of a farming community in the "Old Country," Dominic saw himself as a hard-working laborer qualified for one of the many jobs the booming steel industry had to offer.

We all spring from the merger of two families that literally and figuratively lay the groundwork and shape who we become.

One such position was an entry-level opening on a regional railroad: laying and repairing tracks as a section hand. The work was every bit as grueling as in the fields of his homeland, but the pay was better, the hours more regular and shorter, and he enjoyed the security of his newly formed Brotherhood of Railroad Trainmen.

He eventually rose through the ranks to become a hostler, a yard engineer responsible for piloting locomotives coming off the road into the terminal yard, then positioning them for servicing, and repositioning them to go out again.

Life was good. As their family grew, they could afford to build their family dream home, with luxuries like an icebox, a coal-fired furnace, chickens in the yard, and a fruit cellar to store their annual canned vegetables from the backyard garden harvest.

Then suddenly tragedy hit! In 1918, 22 months after my father was born, the Spanish flu swept through the nation, taking my grandmother Paula's life and leaving Dominic a widower and a working father of five (two under the age of three).

Devastated, he found strength in the friendship, affection, and unconditional love of his extended family and community. Cousins, sponsors, and neighbors offered to care for each of the children, one here and another there.

Going to work every day, while mourning Paula, he visited each child when possible, assuring them of his love for them, and doing what he could to provide for their needs. This was the family's "normal" life for eight years until 1926 when Dominic remarried and moved everyone back home.

Viktor Frankl, the Austrian psychiatrist and a Holocaust survivor, wrote, "Forces beyond your control can take away everything you possess except one thing, your freedom to choose how you will respond to the situation."[2] Dominic's choice was to put one foot in front of the other, one day at a time, stubbornly going forward with persistence, resilience, and character. The family values instilled in him through the love and wisdom of his parents and their parents before them, drove him forward. These foundational values have, for centuries, driven men and women to create progress that benefits both their families and their nations.

Through this experience, Dominic expanded on his familial wisdom by leaving behind the conventional wisdom of his homeland—risking everything to move an ocean and a continent away. He made a new start in an unfamiliar world, adapted to a radically different and evolving socioeconomic environment, leaned on his newly formed and expanded network of family and friends, and ultimately turned his vision of reuniting his loved ones into reality.

The slow and steady patriarch finished his life the same way he lived it: working every day, putting one foot in front of the other, until retiring on a dependable railroad pension. Reaching his ultimate goal of raising and keeping his family together, he passed away at home surrounded by those he loved.

Pacentro, Italy – April 5, 1911

My maternal grandparents, Rocco and Mary, came from a less rural area of their homeland and were on the opposite end of Galbraith's entrepreneur dichotomy. Family grocers in the "Old Country," they set up a storefront in their new home in the same Ohio town as my father's parents, across the street from a steel mill.

Their timing was good. Their store quickly became a convenient neighborhood place to shop. Each year they did a little better financially, and before long they were living comfortably. As the Roaring '20s got underway, the sky was the limit. With the help of a local bank, they made a down payment on a neighborhood single-family home to rent and then another. Eventually they owned properties on several city blocks. With store and rental income flowing, local notoriety followed Rocco's business success. He was a bigger-than-life personality, entertaining guests in his and Mary's grand new home and hosting elegant wedding receptions for their oldest children. He led the annual Italian Day parade riding on a white horse.

But the success didn't last. The effects of Prohibition and the Great Depression, two economic tidal waves in a row, all but wiped them out financially. Federal law shut down their high margin wine business, and failed banks led to the collapse of the real estate market.

Rags to riches are the stories we love, but more common and far less enthralling are stories that begin in wealth and end in struggle. Entrepreneurs lured to the possibility of no ceiling often find themselves with no floor.

They were close to broke, but not broken. Like every other trial and error, you can either learn from it or repeat the same mistakes. Though things were terribly slow, the locals who were fortunate enough to avoid the soup lines of the time still had to eat. And though the inventory was sparce and customers few, Rocco and Mary's struggling grocery business squeaked by.

> *Entrepreneurs lured to the possibility of no ceiling often find themselves with no floor.*

Their children who married during those years did so on their own. No big weddings or starter-home gifts. Living with their parents for a while was the new normal. As my mother would wisely remind me later during unpleasant times, "This too will pass." And so they did.

Within ten years, Rocco and Mary had another new family business literally up and rolling. Along with their two sons (my uncles), the family established themselves as dependable heavy-duty truck haulers, serving the needs of one of the country's busy steel mills supporting the World War II effort.

Rising market demands led to a surge in trucking contracts, necessitating an expanded fleet, more drivers, and preparation for continued growth. Everything was moving forward smoothly—until they also faced sudden tragedy. Richie, their entrepreneurial son poised to succeed Rocco, was killed in a freak auto accident. Without his energy and leadership, the competition eventually prevailed.

Twenty-five years later, in one of the final conversations I had with my grandfather before he passed away, he was excited to tell me about a business model he had developed. Long before United Parcel Service was known to provide such a thing in his area, he imagined a local small-package delivery service. He talked about how he and I could work together beginning with one pickup truck, and using the profits to buy another, and another...

Once an entrepreneur, always an entrepreneur. His vision, resilience, and drive reflected the familial wisdom passed down to him through generations—wisdom that he, in turn, passed on to his children.

Youngstown, OH – August 14, 1941

The day they married, they were just two kids from the same neighborhood—one raised with a slow-and-steady-wins-the-race mindset, the other taught to be innovative and shoot for the sky. Yet both shared deep roots in love and a strong work ethic.

Over the course of their young lives, my parents, Jim and Ann, experienced firsthand the personal ups and downs of family life at a time of massive, unprecedented macroeconomic events. Their generation experienced the boom of the 1920s, the bust of the Great Depression, the shock of World War II, and the peace and prosperity of the 1950s. It was an emotional, social, and economic roller coaster like no other. During the darkest times, all they had to rely on was their love of family, the wisdom they inherited and experienced, and the good the conventional wisdom of their day had to offer.

Following in his father's footsteps, Jim worked for the same railroad, in the same role, with the same steady paycheck. Ann, the adventurous young entrepreneur in her 20s, partnered with two other like-minded women and opened and operated a beauty shop in the busiest part of downtown. The couple was the perfect balance of Galbraith's two synergizing forces of hard work and aspirations.

> *It was an emotional, social, and economic roller coaster like no other.*

During the war years, with two stable income sources, the young couple was fortunate to save enough to build a home for their growing family. By the end of WWII, they were among those blessed to live the American Dream. Family love + Slow-and-steady meets Sky's-the-limit wisdom + Peace and economic prosperity = The perfect formula for building family wealth.

As more children were born, they added another bedroom, and a first-floor storefront salon. Jim, motivated by the demands of educating my brothers and me, supplemented the family income by tapping into his wife's enterprising spirit. The local school district had a need for independent contractors to drive physically and mentally challenged children directly to and from their homes and schools. My dad's first contract involved using the family station wagon to transport four students to and from school before and after his regular shifts on the railroad.

Unknowingly, a multigenerational family enterprise was launched.

Campbell, OH – July 26, 1970

My siblings and I grew up immersed in our parents' kitchen table conversations. (As an Italian family, we usually ate in the kitchen, except on Sundays and holidays.) The discussions ranged from typical family life events to insights on running a railroad, operating a beauty salon, and transporting special needs children to and from school. As the years flew by and my brothers and I became of age to qualify for our chauffeurs' licenses, our dad added more routes, providing each of us with part-time driver jobs and vehicles while studying at our local college. This continued until we were all out on our own.

Youngstown, OH – June 1, 1982

When our father retired, two of my brothers picked up the contracts and began employing extended family members, friends, and acquaintances as drivers. Then opportunity knocked! Like their trucking company uncles before them, my brothers did some research and discovered how the school board might benefit from engaging a single formal contractor for all 1,200 special needs students currently served by dozens of independent "handshake" contractors.

The formal contract was awarded to them on the premise that a professionally managed school bus company could better serve the community with a more rigorous safety and efficiency compliance regimen. At this point, early in my career, it called for all hands on deck to be able to meet the terms of the contract before the first student was bused to school in September.

This opportunity for our family also allowed me to put my experience and skills to the test by contributing to a significant entrepreneurial endeavor in real time. And tested we were—facing the challenge of transforming a company with just a handful of vehicles transporting a few dozen students into one with over 40 specially equipped school buses serving well over a thousand students—all in under 90 days.

My father, two brothers, and I instinctively committed to all-in, no-turning-back weekly meetings. It was a trial by fire for all of us. As the saying goes, "Nothing motivates like a deadline." The experience was harrowing, involving major tasks such as arranging financing, procuring buses, passing inspections, hiring and training drivers, and designing and testing routes. On top of that, we had to manage countless details related to business administration and human resources while ensuring compliance with a government entity.

They are the heirs to a legacy of love and wisdom carefully built by those who came before them.

I cannot say everything went smoothly that first day, but the terms of the contract were met, and the company has continued to grow ever since. What started as a side job has transformed into an innovative, industry-changing, award-winning enterprise. Today, it continues to expand, meeting the modern demand for specialized door-to-door transportation services and consulting.

It stands as a prime example of collective family love and wisdom in action.

Youngstown, Warren, Columbus, and Cleveland, OH – November 28, 2024

Today, my nephews and nieces are preparing to take the baton from their fathers and uncles. Each have grown up at the family business kitchen table, learning from their entrepreneurial parents and grandparents. They have worked from the bottom up in various roles (driving, operations, logistics, management, contracts, human resources, finance, and just about every other job needed to be done to sustain a family-owned and -operated enterprise).

Like every other member of an intergenerational, generative family, they are the heirs to a legacy of love and wisdom carefully built by those who came before them. Where they take it from here is entirely up to them.

Now, let's talk about money.

4

SHOW ME
THE MONEY

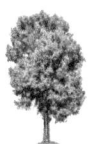

*"I've been rich, and I've been poor,
and rich is better."*

ATTRIBUTED OFTEN TO MAE WEST

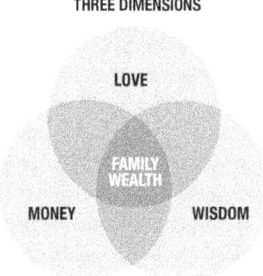

THREE DIMENSIONS

LOVE

FAMILY WEALTH

MONEY · WISDOM

n the movie *Jerry Maguire*, Jerry (played by Tom Cruise),
a sports agent, is on the phone with Rod Tidwell, a rising
football star portrayed by Cuba Gooding Jr. At a pivotal
moment, Jerry asks Rod, "What can I do for you?"

Rod is at home in his kitchen, hanging with his wife and

kids, music blaring. "It's a very personal, very important thing," Tidwell says. "Hell, it's a family motto. Are you ready …?"

He turns down the music: "Here it is," he says quietly. "Show me the money."[1]

"Show me the money"—Tidwell's aphorism catapulted *Jerry Maguire* to movie immortality. All due to the underlying message: Financial opportunity could enhance the lifestyles of the people he loved the most. Rod loved his family and had the wisdom to know this was his opportunity to have the financial means to take his family lifestyle to the next level. As viewers, we could relate to Rod's focus on what truly mattered most to him. The money Rod Tidwell's family was about to come into would no doubt be life-changing, enabling them to cross the threshold from Accumulators to Harvesters.

Tijuana, Mexico – October 22, 2022

In one of the poorest sections of Tijuana, Mexico, a single young mother of two small children had lived with the unrelenting daily fears of not having enough money. She had often wondered what would become of her small struggling family. She was making $85 a week, her thoughts consumed by the very basics of life—food and shelter. She and her two children were living in a one-room makeshift structure (approximately 10 feet by 10 feet) constructed from scrap lumber, with a dirt floor and a roof of old blankets and discarded tarps that leaked when it rained. An old single mattress served as the family's only bed and piece of furniture.

This family was living on unconditional love and enough wisdom to make it from day to day trying to do what is right but with barely enough money to survive. Somehow, she got by. She was fortunate to be able to leave her children with friends or neighbors in a similar plight, while she worked, returning the favor when she could.

Over time a relationship developed with a friendly (one of C.S. Lewis' four types of loves) coworker, a young man no better off but with a similar paycheck. He developed an affection for her and her children and treated them as his own. Eventually, they fell in love (eros), and it wasn't long before they had two more children, making their cramped quarters even tighter. Scrimping to make ends meet day to day, they chose to use their company's $125 per year

Financial opportunity could enhance the lifestyles of the people he loved the most.

December bonuses ($250 collectively) to buy cement and cinder blocks to build a foundation for a permanent house against a steep downward slope on one side of the property.

Six years and six combined bonuses later, the narrow walls had risen nearly as high as the original lot's slope, with plans to add more rows and a permanent roof. If all went well, they estimated another six to ten years to complete the structure.

Then, a miracle happened … or I should say, Build A Miracle (BAM) happened. BAM is a small San Diego-based family-operated charity (another type of love) funded completely by the time and efforts of the founding family and donations of a network of local families, individuals, students, parishioners, and community groups interested in helping as many families as possible in this impoverished community. Numbering more than 500 families to date and still counting.

BAM's charitable model is unique in that its all-volunteer workforce includes community service requirements from the families being helped, introducing them to self-sustaining, personal development and a community-building mindset and lifestyle. The BAM leadership includes the founding family, local Tijuana community activists, and families who are either awaiting or have received homes over the years. They identify, prepare, and engage qualified families—those committed to working their way forward—and match them with donor sponsors. These sponsors finance and actively help construct permanent homes on "build days," replacing the squalor in which the identified families are currently living.

Our Tijuana family of six is one of them. After their required community service (all families selected to receive a home commit to a minimum of 200 hours of service both before and after they move in), with all the building materials delivered to the site and an army of volunteers on hand, not only was the first floor completed but a second floor added, roofed in, and made move-in ready in a matter of weeks. In its completed state, it featured three bedrooms, a family room/kitchen, a full bath, insulated walls, running water, electricity, and was fully furnished—all for under $20,000.

These homes also open the door to something once unattainable: the chance for families to grow their wisdom and resilience.

One year after the day they were presented with their new home, as part of the BAM process, the family took the opportunity to show their gratitude to all those who had participated in building their miracle. They read the following handwritten note in Spanish (translated to English in the donors' and volunteers' presence, and again here).

> To: The most special people in our lives (names of the donors)
> From: The family that loves you the most (their name here)
> Sunday, November 19, 2023
> 1st anniversary in our home.
>
> Thank you so much.
> Hello, have a good and blessed day dear (donors' names), we hope you are feeling well, full of health and blessings.
> Today is a very special day because on this day we are completing one year in our home that we know was possible thanks to all your kindness. The dream of having a roof for our children came true.
> You fulfilled it and, though sometimes I feel like I'm still dreaming, I realize that I already live in the reality that God filled our souls with blessing by putting everyone at the BAM Community Center in our lives. There they have taught us so many things and the most special is helping those who need it most.
> With all our hearts we hope that during these holidays you have a wonderful time with the beings you love most that God knows everything you deserve, today, tomorrow, and always.
> May God remain by your side this Christmas, always giving you LOVE, health and much happiness.
> We say goodbye, but we hope to see each other again very soon, our Angels, we appreciate them very much.

The donors and volunteers also had the opportunity to

vocalize their gratitude for being part of such a wonderful miracle. And as grateful as the receiving family was, and as dramatically as their life has been changed, those who helped make it all possible went on to state in a variety of ways how they were not sure who got the most from the experience. They relayed their own experiences in the process as life-changing, with a greater appreciation for their privileged situation and a greater desire to do more to help others. There wasn't a dry eye in the place. Love, wisdom, and money in action indeed.

Surprisingly, the greatest miracle BAM is creating isn't just the new homes—they're building new lifestyles and fostering outlooks that rise above despair. These homes also open the door to something once unattainable: the chance for families to grow their wisdom and resilience, opportunities that were impossible under their former living conditions.

Whether you are a family in Tijuana making ends meet and escaping poverty, the Tidwells reaching for financial independence at the height of a career, or an entrepreneurial family who has amassed more capital than you will ever need to support your lifestyle, starting out as an Accumulator, your main concern was financial security. However, once you cross the threshold of financial freedom—where you have more money than necessary to support your lifestyle—you, as family fiduciary, are faced with the question, "Now what?" As Cindi Lauper puts it, "Money changes everything."

MONEY AND THE ESSENCE OF FAMILY WEALTH

Surplus income and assets, beyond lifestyle needs, give you and your family the capacity to express who you are as individuals and as a family unit: what you value, who you want to become, and how you intend to impact the world.

It is important to realize that what you do with your wealth at this juncture, even if it's doing nothing at all, will impact others who are watching. Adam Smith, often referred to as the father of modern economics, stated that even though it may or may not be true, "wealth and greatness are often regarded with the [kind of] respect and admiration which are due only to wisdom and virtue."

Love, wisdom, and money in action are the essence of healthy family wealth and its fundamental foundation.

Beyond financial security, money is an expressive tool. The way you deploy it, whether within or outside the family, becomes a manifestation, broadcaster, and amplifier of what you and your family value, rooted in the wisdom passed down through generations. Its power can be infinitely useful to you and those around you, or intoxicating to the point of taking on a life of its own.

To use a phrase coined by Harvard University's Clayton Christensen, the "job to be done" as a family fiduciary is first and foremost to be an informed instrument of unconditional love in the family. Within the human condition, such authentic love and caring wisdom allows a family to persevere over an extended period.

Francis de Sales, the early 17th-century Roman Catholic bishop of Geneva, Switzerland, wrote these words of wisdom: "You learn to speak by speaking, to study by studying, to run by running, to work by working; and just so you learn to love …

by loving. … Begin as a mere apprentice, and the very power of love will lead you on to become a master in the art." This concept suggests that if you find yourself as an apprentice steward, the very powers of love and wisdom can guide you to master the art of stewardship.

What's true for the family members from Mexico, and those who sponsor them, is true for all families—whatever your status, financial wealth, and opportunity. Love, wisdom, and money in action are the essence of healthy family wealth and its fundamental foundation. Without all three, your family is at a disadvantage, possibly even in jeopardy. With them, your family is empowered to be all it can be. Deep love paired with practical wisdom provides a steady compass for a family, guiding them toward their true north amid a rapidly changing world. Money gives you the liberty to move forward on your own path at your own pace.

Money gives you the liberty to move forward on your own path at your own pace.

While both love and wisdom tend to be abstract and undefinable, you know them when you see them. They are observed and measured in the action they inspire and revealed in how you spend your money. James Hughes, author of *Family Wealth—Keeping It in the Family*, was the first to identify family wealth as a combination of human capital (love), intellectual capital (wisdom), and financial capital (money).

"A family that's nothing but quantitative capital," he writes, "is toast."[2]

Yet without money, building family wealth can be an endless struggle.

From this perspective, though money changes everything, money is not the problem. It's focusing on money alone that can trip you up. Sometimes it is simply greed. And greed is blinding. The idea of "more" can capture the human imagination and paralyze you, not allowing you to do what's best for you and the long-term health of your family. I once heard it said that greed is nothing more than misplaced love. It can also be seen as the opposite of love. Genuine love for others, with a focus on their best interests, helps keep money in its proper place—enhancing its purpose and usefulness.

In the opening story of this book, the family did not sell their appreciated stock. That's not to say they were greedy. The allure of making more money significantly clouded their vision of what the money could do for themselves and others under their current circumstances. Money can blind even the best of us.

That is why it's critical to know who you are and what you want. When you do, it is easier to adopt the wry parody "The lack of money is the root of all evil."[3] Along the same lines, Yuval Noah Harari writes in his book *Sapiens*, that far from being the root of all evil, "money is the most universal and most efficient system of mutual trust ever devised."[4] Money works worldwide, and it works for you in situations that without it you have no means of getting things done.

It is the handiest of tools when you know how to use it, perhaps one of the greatest inventions of all time. Money is a universal medium of exchange that enables people to convert almost everything into almost anything else. In other words, money is fungible. Apply it as you desire. And money can enable you not merely to turn one thing into another, but to store your financial wealth for as long as you want, and transport it to any place you choose.

Money is as close as we can come to an almost universally agreed-upon measure of value. We trade our labor and ideas for it, and in turn trade it for what we want but do not have. To say it in another way, what you do with your money is an expression of who your family is, who it can be, and how it chooses to influence the world.

What you do with your money is an expression of who your family is, who it can be, and how it chooses to influence the world.

Stating the patently obvious: Money is clearly essential for living, and it's just as essential to see money clearly for what it is instead of letting it blind you to what it can never be. Like any other tool, such as a chain saw, when used properly you can complete the job to be done quickly and efficiently. Used improperly, you can do irreparable damage.

Now that we've placed money, the powerful tool that it is, in its proper perspective, it's time to look more deeply into who you are and what you want for yourself and your family. In the next chapters, we'll delve into the practical applications of systematically nurturing your family wealth. Together, we'll explore how to integrate your unique blend of love, wisdom, and money. Through real-life scenarios, you'll gain actionable insights to guide you in your role as a family fiduciary, helping your family wealth reach its fullest potential.

5

HOW HARD CAN IT BE?

"Life is like a game. First you learn the rules, and then you play to win."

ATTRIBUTED TO ALBERT EINSTEIN

A s we've seen in earlier chapters, significant financial wealth brings increased complexity in both financial management and family dynamics. While it's natural to wish for simplicity, true simplicity—the kind that brings clarity and focus—can only be achieved by first navigating and understanding those complexities. To paraphrase Supreme Court Justice Oliver Wendell Holmes, "I would give my life for the simplicity that lies on the other side of complexity." It's not about avoiding the hard work; it's about using that effort to distill what truly matters.

Cleveland, OH – August 8, 1982

Before entering the financial services industry, I avoided what

I saw as the unnecessary and burdensome complexities of life. That was the case until I faced the task of assisting my parents and brothers with their business succession plan. I asked myself, *Why does it have to be so complicated?* I felt there had to be a way to simplify things so everyone involved could understand and make informed decisions.

Simplify. Simplify. Simplify. That became my mission in everything I did. I realized that no matter how complex the system, breaking it down into understandable steps was the key to informed

It's not about avoiding the hard work; it's about using that effort to distill what truly matters.

decisions and smoother outcomes. Once I saw the bigger picture, the chaos started to make sense, and I could help others navigate it with clarity. In fact, it felt eerily similar to my days as an air traffic controller.

When you think about it, the goal of family wealth protection and growth can be simple: maintain a healthy balance of love, wisdom, and money while keeping all the stakeholders engaged and enjoying the process.

Sounds like it could be a good game to me. But talk about complicated.

LIFESTYLE

For starters, entrepreneurs not only think outside the box—they live outside the box of conventional wisdom. They willingly take on risks and uncertainty that could jeopardize family finances and lifestyle. Initially, it's all about generating enough income to meet the family's needs while maintaining enough cash flow to keep the business running. As income increases, the challenge shifts to making enough to support the lifestyle, pay taxes, and continue growing.

PORTFOLIO

Throughout this journey, the demand for more capital feels relentless. Whether borrowing from others or reinvesting in the business, both come at the price of interest, taxes—or both. Adding to this is the competition for familial lifestyle capital: homes, cars, children's education, weddings, and all the other demands that define an abundant family life.

LEGACY

An abundant family life is not just about finances—it's shaped by day-to-day interactions and how you balance your efforts between business and family. These moments become the foundation of how you'll be remembered—your legacy. Another dimension of this legacy is reflected in how you plan for and transfer the financial resources you've accumulated and the message they send to those who follow.

THE FAMILY WEALTH GAME^{SM}

With unconditional love and collective wisdom as our guides, we found that managing family financial wealth could be played as one big game made up of three underlying games.

As we have learned, in its most basic form the family wealth game is as simple as ABC and 123: The ABCs of love, wisdom, money, and the 123s of lifestyle, portfolio, legacy.

Del Cerro, CA – July 7, 2008

An entrepreneurial spouse in her mid-80s sat in her estate planning attorney's office at her wits' end. Her husband, a vibrant and successful entrepreneur for many decades, recently had a life-threatening stroke. Though he was hanging on, the damage had been done. It was highly unlikely he would ever regain competency.

She asked her trusted advisor, "What do I do now?" She and her husband had an estate of more than $13 million[A] with numerous real estate and business holdings. Now it was all in her lap. Because the couple often talked about business, she was familiar with almost all the holdings they had accumulated, but more as a confidant and observer than as a hands-on manager.

Despite the sudden tragedy, she was fortunate. Their legal documents consisting of multiple trusts, LLCs, powers of attorney, and the like were in order. Still, she needed assistance. Theirs was a complicated portfolio of closely-held assets where leases and contracts had to be reviewed and renegotiated, and properties had been sold with notes of various terms and maturity dates that were set to come up for renewal or liquidation. She was an entrepreneurial spouse who, though not involved in the management of the family enterprise, was emotionally intelligent and what some people call "street-smart." She understood what was at stake and was more than capable of making family fiduciary decisions.

Their son and his wife, along with their five adult grandchildren, lived out of state. He was an accomplished entrepreneurial

---

[A] In 2008, $13 million had a purchasing power of approximately $19.3 million in 2024.

craftsman but unfamiliar with intricacies associated with his parents' various business holdings and legal commitments. When he asked how he might help, he added, "I will do what I can, but I am in no position to drop everything and move to California to run things." Their daughter, employed and living on her own, was never interested in the family business activities. Divorced, she had her hands full with three adult children who were all struggling financially.

> *Entrepreneurs not only think outside the box—they live outside the box of conventional wisdom.*

The estate attorney, who was familiar with our process, referred the matriarch to our firm. When we first met, I explained to her, "All your decisions will fall into three distinct categories, like the three different card games of the family board game Tripoley. A decision in one category will have an impact on the other two and ultimately affect your total score. Just like the game, doing well at all three increases your chances to win and get what you want."

She said, "That's it?"

I replied, "That's it."

She embraced the process and wanted to get started immediately.

THE FAMILY WEALTH GAME:^{SM} LIFESTYLE, PORTFOLIO, LEGACY^{SM}

Just as love, wisdom, and money are the essential driving forces behind family wealth, lifestyle cash-flow control, portfolio asset management, and legacy estate planning are the essential activities necessary to oversee all things personally financial. We call it the Family Wealth Game,^{SM} in which all your plans are in one easy-to-manage program. The games were developed along the lines of a Ted Turner quote, "If I have a manager who has all the information they need in front of them and can't make a decision in twenty minutes ... I'll fire them."

The game is predicated on the idea that you can only make good decisions when you have all the information you need in front of you. The game is made up of three one-page presentations, or gameboards, displaying all pertinent information in a simple format to facilitate decision-making in each of the three categories: Lifestyle, Portfolio, and Legacy. Players (family fiduciaries, family members, and advisors) can view each game individually, or all three at the same time.

All your decisions will fall into three distinct categories.

No, we do not fire our clients if it takes longer than twenty minutes to decide. However, the format helps them make progress at their own pace while maintaining a sense of urgency. They are free to use the games to ask questions; brainstorm; collaborate; digest various scenario strategies, tactics, and desired outcomes; understand everything; and then decide how to proceed.

Within a year, with all the information she needed in front of her in a usable format (though not without her share of stress), our client undoubtedly was in control of daily decisions and developing her vision for the future.

LET THE GAMES BEGIN

We met regularly together, and she monitored her family's affairs methodically. She had a firm grasp of the bigger picture.

Within her three-game context, she confidently interacted with her family's business partners and individual professional specialists: CPA, attorneys, real estate agents, bankers, and investment advisors. Her husband had single-handedly chosen and engaged his partners and advisors in a typical "break-fix," as-needed manner. All of them accurately described their roles relevant to their expertise, but none of them were privy to the complete picture in the context of the grand scheme of things. This is one of the key challenges of a family fiduciary. You have an estate planning attorney, a CPA, and a wealth manager. You also may have personal and commercial real estate agents, a business broker or investment banker, or any number of other specialized professionals to help you manage it all.

Each specialist's expertise is critical to protecting and building your family wealth in their area of specialization. And naturally, when faced with a question outside their area of focus, they tend to filter their response through the lens with which they view the world. And rightfully so. It would be inappropriate to assume they were schooled in also coordinating an entire team of other specialty advisors on your behalf. This leaves the challenge of winning the big game squarely on your shoulders as the family fiduciary steward.

This widow saw her husband's approach to business as similar to the lesson depicted in the legendary Indian parable about five blind men trying to describe an elephant by touch from their own point of view. [1] She felt she had to step back and consider all the issues in conjunction with the entire family enterprise.

Therein lies the power of the game: aligning Lifestyle, Portfolio, and Legacy strategies in a coordinated way that enables her to begin with the end in mind. From a social network perspective, this approach helps her integrate and fine-tune her advisory team to align with her vision, values, and goals, ensuring thoughtful decision-making. After a short while, with this mindset she was prepared to confidently go from asking, "What can I do now?" to "What shall I do next?"

But life seldom stays like that for long.

San Diego, CA – August 25, 2010

FAMILY WEALTH CONTINUUM

A little over two years after her husband's stroke, he passed away. During that time, she transitioned from being the supportive wife of a lifelong entrepreneur to a full-time caregiver and family fiduciary steward. As the surviving spouse and successor trustee of the family trust, she faced the daunting challenge of settling her husband's estate.

Living trusts, especially in community property states like California, are an excellent way for married couples to hold title. They avoid the lengthy, expensive, and public probate process by holding all assets in one place, making the estate settlement process private and organized. While trusts provide flexibility during life and ensure organized affairs, they don't eliminate all challenges. Every estate, even one held in trust, must still go through the estate settlement process—a topic explored in a later chapter.

Our surviving spouse not only had to grieve the loss of her lifelong soulmate and business partner but also navigate the pressures, expenses, and complex decisions of trust administration. She began to realize it was now up to her to prepare her family for when she would no longer be around. With her family wealth Lifestyle, Portfolio, and Legacy plans in progress, she was as prepared as any survivor could be for this life event. Having these strategies well in hand made the transition, though still radical, much more manageable.

This experience also positioned her as the family fiduciary, focusing her attention on their two-part legacy estate plan—his and hers. It was a two-year process but managing the family wealth game helped her finalize her own legacy estate plan while facing "the most stressful life event of all." (For more on this subject, see my book *The Coming Widow Boom: What You and Your Loved Ones Can Do to Prepare for the Unthinkable*.)

San Diego, CA – August 17, 2013

The estate planning attorney who referred our matriarch family fiduciary once told me, "People don't always die in order."

Within three years of her husband's passing and after her new way of life as a single surviving spouse became somewhat normal, our surviving spouse's daughter died within a few months of being diagnosed with cancer. More grief struck our matriarch, the loss of a child, among the most stressful life events of all. And with that, there was yet another estate to settle. As we've learned, even the best-laid plans can be difficult to navigate, and her daughter's family dynamic was no exception. As emotionally difficult as it was, settling her daughter's modest financial estate was relatively straightforward. However, our matriarch began to think about the implications her daughter's passing might have on the distribution of her own estate plan.

This leaves the challenge of winning the big game squarely on your shoulders as the family fiduciary steward.

Her and her husband's original intent was to divide their estate equally between their daughter and son. However, with her daughter now gone—leaving no spouse and two of her daughter's three children struggling and financially unsophisticated—she worried outright gifts might do more harm than good. Viewing her other grandchildren in this new light, she felt her son's children were better equipped to handle such largesse. She asked her attorney, "How can I provide for both sets of families while accounting for their different levels of financial competency?"

One legal hurdle was her husband's share of the estate was held in an irrevocable trust. The trust terms, set years earlier, required his daughter's share to go outright to her children. Her experienced estate planning attorney explained, "While you cannot change the terms of your husband's trust, you have the limited power to direct your living trust to purchase assets from the irrevocable trust in exchange for interest-bearing notes."

Implementing this strategy would address her daughter's

children's needs without burdening them with the responsibility of managing the properties. By transferring the properties to her living trust instead of leaving them in her husband's irrevocable trust, she would retain control over the dispositive provisions.

Of course, there was much more to the process. The simple point of this case is, a surviving spouse as trustee of both her and her husband's trusts had the flexibility to legally and morally modify both estates to better meet her family's needs and best interests as circumstances changed.

FAMILY WEALTH CONTINUUM: HEIR

As our surviving spouse immersed herself in the legacy game, she developed a better feeling for her role as a family fiduciary. Knowing she would eventually pass the baton to the next fiduciary, she thought about what she might do to prepare her son.

After experiencing the difficulties of what we refer to as the "first-time buyer's syndrome" experienced by most successor trustees, she thought it wise to give her son a chance to try it on for size before being thrust into the role by her death or disability. So, she resigned as successor trustee of her husband's trust (the one with his half of their community property) and replaced herself with her son.

Unfamiliar with the task, the son was eager to learn all he could about the role of trustee. And what a job he did! His methodical, one-foot-in-front-of-the-other style fit perfectly with his definitive legal fiduciary duties. His love for the family was evident as he began preparing his nephews—even those somewhat estranged—for the art and science of managing more money than they had ever handled. It was enough, if they were prudent, to provide for themselves and their families for a lifetime. Within a few months of the son accepting the successor trustee responsibilities of his father's half of the estate, his mother passed away. I have heard it said that some people can hang on to life long enough to know they have done everything

Even the best-laid plans can be difficult to navigate.

possible for those they care about who follow to take it from there. Our surviving spouse—family fiduciary steward matriarch—certainly did. And, even with only a few months behind the wheel as family fiduciary successor trustee, her son took over as a better prepared family fiduciary steward heir—and next-in-line patriarch.

NAVIGATING WEALTH WITH CLARITY

You have now completed a full cycle through one generational revolution of a family's wealth continuum story. Just as spring brings growth, summer flourishing, fall maturity, and winter the appearance of death, I hope it is clear that all your family wealth continuum tree needs to thrive and regenerate is a healthy environment of love, wisdom, and a commitment to playing the games to win.

In the next three chapters, we will explore real-life examples of how other families have faced and overcome obstacles. These stories will delve into the nuances of each of the three key games, offering insights into how families have leveraged their values, vision, love, and wisdom as driving forces in making thoughtful, dynamic, and financially sound decisions to achieve their goals.

You will discover how streamlining your approach can systematically and habitually engage family members and advisors. By simplifying complexity, mitigating fear and stress, reducing risks and taxes, and fostering clarity, you'll increase the likelihood of reaching your goals—and better position future generations to achieve theirs.

6

THE LIFESTYLE CASH FLOW GAME

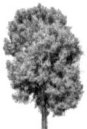

*"When your outgo exceeds your income,
then your upkeep will be your downfall."*

ATTRIBUTED TO BILL EARLE

W e've seen throughout the previous chapters how family finances can stir up emotions—whether it's the pressure of preserving a legacy, the complexities of navigating a crisis, or making long-term investment decisions. The stories shared illustrate just how overwhelming these situations can be, often leading to clouded decision-making.

Research shows that gamifying tasks can tap into our natural desires for motivation, competition, and reward. According to *Forbes*, gamification engages the brain's problem-solving centers, making abstract financial concepts more tangible and giving a sense of progress and control.[1] Game designer Jane

McGonigal also emphasizes that games foster a growth mindset, or a "challenge mindset," helping individuals tackle tasks with persistence and resilience.[2]

Please do not let the simplicity of the gameboards––which are simply abstract representations of the bigger picture—fool you. The games featured in this chapter and the chapters to come are designed for the entire family and other trusted individuals to play so each person, as financially sophisticated or unsophisticated as they may be, can identify big-picture family wealth matters in a relatable way.

Each of the three gameboards provides a framework for oversight, interaction, and discussion in the key areas of family financial wealth management: Lifestyle, Portfolio, and Legacy. Individually, the games allow you to focus on the critical aspects of each area. Together, they offer a triangulated view of the big picture, combining concrete information with the broader perspective needed to make better strategic and tactical decisions.

People learn by watching others. By playing games and watching those who are making decisions, this type of learning helps establish generative wealth habits in next-generation participants. The more deeply engaged the observers are, and the broader their understanding, the more likely they are to become effective players when it's their turn to make decisions. The format encourages active involvement from all participants, drawing on their unique perspectives, interests, and skills. Like any family board game, this personal engagement keeps everyone invested in the process. For ease of use, all three gameboards follow the same simple format, while addressing the different aspects of family financial wealth. Each gameboard is divided into three sections: the top (resources); the middle (commitments); and the bottom (result scores), which indicates how well you're performing in each game.

The gameboards highlight and summarize the key factors that can either enrich or detract from your financial position. The interaction between the various games adds elements of challenge and fun that are crucial to keeping players in the game. In this chapter, we will focus exclusively on income sources and expenditures, which make up the very heart of the Lifestyle Cash Flow game.

LIFESTYLE INCOME, DISBURSEMENTS, BUDGETS, AND SPENDING PLANS

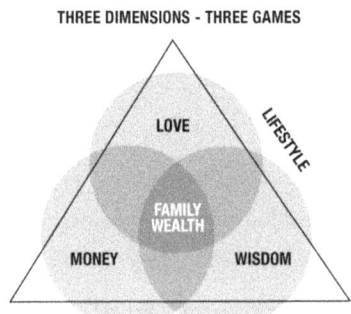

The most basic family financial plan is a household budget. Some financial advisors now refer to it as a "spending plan." Whatever you call it, how you manage your family's household income and disbursements to support your family lifestyle is a function of your lifestyle cash flow.

Lifestyle cash flow refers to the actual movement of money

through the family's personal accounts on a daily, weekly, monthly, or yearly basis. As many businesspeople understand, you can have a reasonable budget but still fall dangerously short of cash flow due to events beyond your control. Budgets are projections of what you intend to make and spend and are necessary tools for establishing benchmarks and measuring progress. Managing cash flow has to do with the actual timing and decision-making required for effective budget implementation.

Research shows that gamifying tasks can tap into our natural desires for motivation, competition, and reward.

If the heating and air conditioning unit in your home (a big-ticket item) suddenly goes out before its planned life expectancy, even though you may have budgeted for it, you still may run into a cash flow problem. It's one that can be solved relatively simply if you have all the cash set aside for the event; it's more cumbersome and restrictive if you do not have the cash and are forced to borrow or sacrifice some other expenditure to pay for it.

EXTREME EXAMPLES

Robert T. Kiyosaki, author of *Rich Dad Poor Dad* and creator of the board game CASHFLOW, tells the story of how he chose to live in his car to minimize cash flow disbursements and devote the bulk of his surplus income to build enough capital to generate enough passive income sufficient to pay the rent for an apartment.[3]

Another example is a family in the retail business during the

Great Recession of 2008, who found their $50,000[A] per month lifestyle income reduced to a negative $20,000 per month.[B]

Immediate lifestyle sacrifices can be painful, but your cash flow habits carry implications far beyond everyday conveniences. For entrepreneurial families with operating businesses or rental real estate (like my grandfather Rocco), the challenge often lies in managing lifestyle and other expenses—planned or unplanned—that exceed current income. Entrepreneurial family fiduciaries may suddenly face specific cash flow crunches—often temporary but potentially impactful over time, regardless of their position on the family wealth continuum.

How you manage your family's household income and disbursements to support your family lifestyle is a function of your lifestyle cash flow.

La Mesa, CA – March 2, 1990

Early in my advising career, I was introduced to a woman looking for some investment advice. She lived in a modest house in a quiet, lower middle-income neighborhood. She had a tough life but was doing what she could to get what she wanted. Divorced and living alone, she was legally blind but had above-average financial savvy. When we first met, she said, "I have an adult daughter, but we hardly speak anymore." It was obvious there was pain beneath the surface, but I did not know what.

[A] In 2008, $50,000 had purchasing power of approximately $74,000 in 2024.

[B] In 2008, negative $20,000 had purchasing power of approximately negative $30,000 in 2024.

When I asked her what I could do for her, she replied, "I am not happy with some of my investments and heard that you might have something better." I explained our big-picture approach and asked, "Would you mind sharing everything you have so I can do a thorough assessment first?" She said she trusted the person who introduced us and agreed to share her financial information.

I discovered she owned her home with no mortgage, was living on Social Security, and had so few expenditures there was plenty of surplus income at the end of every month. She had accumulated over $3 million.[C] Most was invested in bonds and conservative securities that were generating monthly income of nearly $15,000[D] ('90 AFR ~8%). From a risk tolerance and investment policy standpoint, I felt there was not much more I could do for her.

When I asked what she planned to do with her money, she said she was going to leave it all to her daughter. "She will need it when I'm gone," she said. Considering their strained relationship, her plan did not make sense. When I asked her daughter about her relationship with her mother, she explained the source of the strain. "I'm living with my boyfriend and my mother doesn't agree with it," she said. "When we do talk, we usually end up arguing and stay away from each other for a while."

It was an incredibly sad situation, two family members who obviously loved each other (albeit not unconditionally), living in a fractured relationship. I felt helpless to fix their relationship. But I knew I could help my client with her plans to pass

---

[C] In 1990, $3 million had purchasing power of approximately $7.4 million in 2024.

[D] In 1990, $15,000 had purchasing power of approximately $37,000 in 2024.

her wealth to her daughter. It dawned on me, though she was saving *all* of her money for her daughter, she was living in a classic Accumulator mode.

The least I could do was give the mother a little clarity about her situation. Her monthly Cash Flow gameboard (simplified) looked something like this:

THE LA MESA FAMILY LIFESTYLE CASH FLOW
MARCH 1990

	+/-	MONTHLY	ANNUALLY
SOURCES **(+)**	Social Security	1,500	18,000
	Portfolio	15,000	180,000
	Total	16,500	198,000
DISBURSEMENTS **(−)**	Lifestyle	3,000	36,000
	Taxes	3,000	36,000
	Total	6,000	72,000
RESULTS **(+)**	Surplus	10,500	126,000

She knew she was saving and investing, but she had not realized she was saving almost double what she was spending on her lifestyle. She was hyper-focused on "save, save, save" and "invest, invest, invest"—and nothing else; she seemed to be less concerned about healing the strained relationship between her and her daughter, whom she obviously loved. The gameboard reflected that. In the mirror of these gameboards you get a clear sense of the way you are acting, and in a sense, you are forced to reconcile what you are doing with what you want to be doing. Whether you do anything about the disconnect or not is up to you.

After that day she and I did very little business together. But we kept in touch for a few years. The last time we spoke, I asked, "How are you and your daughter doing?"

All she said was, "Better."

San Diego, CA – February 3, 1995

A few years later, I was introduced to another widow who was named the "lifetime income" beneficiary of her second husband's trust with assets totaling approximately $1.5 million.[E] Her projected annual income ('93 AFR ~4%) was in the vicinity of $60,000[F] per year. The trust "remainderman" beneficiaries were her deceased spouse's children. Her relationship with them could be characterized as "distant" at best.

She informed us, "I have my own children from my first marriage, and I am interested in helping them."

Immediate lifestyle sacrifices can be painful, but your cash flow habits carry implications far beyond everyday conveniences.

The income from the trust was plenty for her to maintain the lifestyle she had become accustomed to while living with her second husband, but there would not be much surplus for her children.

She asked her attorney, "How can I help my children? There is plenty of money in the trust, and I am the trustee, so what can I do about it?"

"This is an irrevocable trust that cannot be changed," her

[E] In 1995, $1.5 million had purchasing power of approximately $3.1 million in 2024.

[F] In 1995, $60,000 had purchasing power of approximately $125,000 in 2024.

attorney said. "You, as a trustee, are held to a fiduciary standard to act within the intent dictated in the trust document which entitles you only to the income."

She responded, "What if something happens to me that requires more income?"

He went on, "There are health, education, maintenance, and support provisions that permit you to invade the corpus (assets) of the trust under limited circumstances."

"What circumstances?" she asked.

"The trust already provides all the income for your lifestyle education, support, and maintenance needs," he said, "so that only leaves the matter of your health."

To pay for the additional disbursements she began to spend down assets.

"Like what?"

"You know, doctors' appointments, medication, physical therapy, counseling—really anything your doctors prescribe treatment for that's not covered by Medicare or your health insurance plan."

It was amazing after that day the number of maladies she encountered (apparently legitimately!) qualifying as health-related expenses. To pay for the additional disbursements she began to spend down assets. Her attorney, accountant, and I kept detailed records of what were deemed valid expenditures. As trustee, she met her fiduciary responsibility by providing the remainderman beneficiaries (her stepchildren) with the required trust accounting summary at the end of each year. This is a prime example of how increased expenditures can methodically erode assets.

Over time, her trust distribution demands increased,

reaching such a rate that if they continued, they would be unsustainable for her life expectancy. There was a fiscal cliff on the horizon. Her situation describes a typical challenge looming among Harvesters with definitive assets.

When we informed her of the dilemma, she asked, "How long will it last?" Her monthly Cash Flow gameboard (simplified) looked something like this:

TRUST WIDOW FAMILY
LIFESTYLE CASH FLOW
FEBRUARY 1995

	+/-	MONTHLY	ANNUALLY
SOURCES (+)	Trust Portfolio	5,000	60,000
DISBURSEMENTS (-)	Lifestyle	4,000	
	Taxes	1,000	
	Health	10,000	
	Total	15,000	180,000
RESULTS (-)	Deficit	(10,000)	(120,000)

In response to "How long will it last?" we showed her what we have come to call a "Fiscal Cliff Projection." It is a report that represents likely outcomes under a set of reasonable "burn rate" scenario assumptions; it indicates the number of years and months of income she would have until it was gone. For example, considering the scenario above, the report indicated she could expect to arrive at her fiscal cliff and be out of money in approximately eight years and eight months.

When she first saw it, she said, "I'm planning on being

around longer than that!"

Within a few months, her health expenses, and consequently her trust disbursements, began to fluctuate. Some quarters required additional disbursements and others less, which broke the previous pattern of steadily increasing healthcare costs. As her burn rate increased, the cliff drew nearer; as it decreased, it moved farther into the future. Her situation turned into a classic "sinking fund" model, where the fiscal "gas in the tank" is burned until the time there is no more.

She lived the remainder of her life (about 15 years) with one eye on her fiscal cliff and one on her burn rate. She passed away leaving just under $100,000 of "gas in the tank" trust portfolio assets to be passed along to the remainderman beneficiaries. This reflected her unique version of vision, values, and goals in action.

THE FAMILY BURN RATE

All families are different based on who you are, what you need, what you have, and what you want. Your lifestyle spending beyond your basic needs is a series of discretionary choices— family fiduciary choices. These choices fluctuate between the impact you feel your disbursements will make now and what you envision for them later. It's a serious job. The path and plan you choose (your vision), and the commitment and courage to act accordingly (your values), put you in a position to assume control of your family burn rate.

So, what's the secret? In the words of Stephen Covey, "It's easy to say 'no!' when there's a deeper 'yes!' burning inside."[4]

In his book *The Legacy Journey*, Dave Ramsey discusses the concept of "contentment" and the personal exercise that goes along with determining an appropriate burn rate for your family.[5] I have yet to encounter a family who is successful at building financial wealth that has not established their cash flow contentment level, whether consciously or unconsciously.

St. Mother Teresa, the founder of the Missionaries of Charity, was known for her work with the poor in Calcutta. She got by on very little. Her monthly cash flow was nominal; she died with little if any personal financial wealth. Yet, who would argue that she was not content? In contrast, it was reported that when then businessman Donald Trump encountered a cash flow crunch in the late 1980s and turned to his bankers for help, one condition of the loan package was that his family restrict their lifestyle cash flow burn rate to $450,000[G] per month!

The work of managing a family's cash flow requires a mix of prudence, foresight, contentment, and wisdom.

There is no judgment here. Family lifestyles are personal; cash flow control issues are among the most basic of all fiduciary disciplines. For family fiduciaries, managing cash flow with wisdom means not only optimizing returns but also ensuring your family wealth stability. The work of managing a family's cash flow requires a mix of prudence, foresight, contentment, and wisdom.

San Diego, CA – March 15, 2006

Earlier in this chapter, I mentioned a retail business owner

[G] In 1990, $450,000 had purchasing power of approximately $1.1 million in 2024.

client family that experienced a prolonged cash flow crunch because of the impact the Great Recession of 2008 had on their business. Here is what their gameboard looked like between pre-recession 2006 and mid-recession 2008.

THE RETAIL FAMILY
LIFESTYLE CASH FLOW
DECEMBER 2006 (PRE-RECESSION)

	+/-	MONTHLY	ANNUALLY
SOURCES (+)	Business Profits	300,000	3,600,000
DISBURSEMENTS (-)	Lifestyle	50,000	600,000
	Taxes	150,000	1,800,000
	Total	200,000	2,400,000
RESULTS (+)	Surplus	100,000	1,200,000

When we met for their first quarter 2006 review, the family fiduciary said something I was not expecting but will never forget: "Buddy, I have a feeling something really bad is going to happen!" His statement took me by surprise, because the economy appeared to be roaring at the time. To me the economic mood of the country was among the best I had ever seen. How wrong I was!

"I don't know what it is," he said, "but just to be prepared, I have begun to stockpile cash." Here was a seasoned businessman whose opinion I respected immensely, and he was serious. After that conversation, even I sensed a shift was coming. The question became, "Can things really be this good?" As it turned out, they were not.

This is what their family gameboard looked like between 2008 after the implosion and when the smoke began to clear from the recession economy and their industry in 2010.

**THE RETAIL FAMILY
LIFESTYLE CASH FLOW**
DECEMBER 2008 (RECESSION)

	+/-	MONTHLY	ANNUALLY
SOURCES (-)	Business Losses	20,000	240,000
DISBURSEMENTS (-)	Reduced Lifestyle	30,000	
	Taxes	0	
	Total	30,000	360,000
RESULTS (-)	Deficit	(50,000)	(600,000)

Even after severely curtailing their lifestyle, their business and personal disbursements averaged negative $50,000[H] per month for nearly four very long years.

As the recession took hold, the fear of what might happen next was so widespread in the marketplace that the value of nearly everything in the economy became uncertain. Traditional business appraisal methods could no longer be trusted. Several of the largest banks and premier financial institutions collapsed. And negative economic shockwaves were felt all around the globe.

[H] In 2008, negative $50,000 had a purchasing power of approximately negative $74,700 in 2024.

It was a scary time. Fortunately, this family fiduciary, a classic Steward persona, had the vision to prepare for the worst and see it through. And it served him, his family, his employees, and customers well.

I will also never forget the pain I saw in his eyes during those dark days of nurturing the family savings and doing all he could to make it last as long as possible in the face of what felt like never-ending uncertainty. His actions exemplify the central theme of this book: that successful family wealth management is not just about financial expertise, but also about the wise stewardship of resources in times of both prosperity and adversity. This kind of stewardship, grounded in love and wisdom, is what ensures the flourishing of families across generations.

THE COW AND ITS MILK

Lifestyle income, beyond what you earn from employment, is usually a matter of earnings on investments. Whether you call it business profits, dividends, interest, distributions, or simply portfolio income, it can be likened to the milk produced by a cow.

Our next chapter, "The Portfolio Net Worth Game," is dedicated to the care and feeding of your cow.

7

THE PORTFOLIO NET WORTH GAME

*"Know what you own,
and know why you own it."*

PETER LYNCH

For perspective only, recent government data for the top 10% of average household financial wealth ("cow") in the United States can be roughly broken down as follows:[1]
- 90 to 99 percentiles $4,756,716
- 99 to 99.9 percentile $21,827,328
- .01 percentile $158,646,706

Understanding money as a tool, alongside love and wisdom, is essential to building and sustaining your family wealth. These numbers provide context and a wonderful way for you to keep score of how you are doing and measure your progress as time passes. To provide additional insight, government data enables us to approximate the top 10% of US holdings across three major asset categories:[A]

- Marketable Securities 55%
- Real Estate 30%
- Closely Held Businesses 15%

As a footnote to this data, it was also stated that while the Marketable Securities percentage is highest, a great deal of those securities has been purchased as a result of families liquidating their Closely Held Businesses and reinvesting the proceeds into the public markets.

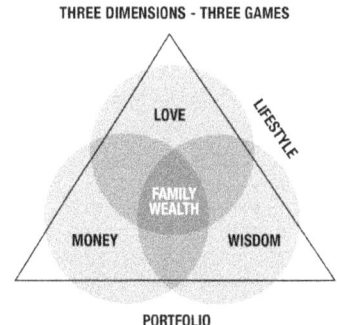

PORTFOLIOS, BALANCE SHEETS, AND NET WORTH

Conventional wisdom has you measuring your financial wealth in terms of net worth:

Assets - Liabilities = Net Worth.

For the sake of the game, as we continue to simplify big-picture planning and family communication, we have found it

---

[A] Interpolated from Federal Reserve Bank statistics 2022.

helpful to step back and view your portfolio "cow" (assets and liabilities) and the kind of impact it can have on the production of "milk."

Here is an oversimplified example:

Question: How much gross income would your family generate from a $1 million asset after making 10% interest payments on a $900,000 loan?

Answer: It all depends on what you do with the $900,000. You could either:

A. Spend it all on lifestyle consumption; the loan becomes debt that reduces your income by $90,000 per year; or

B. Invest it all for a 25% return; the loan becomes leverage increasing your gross income after making loan payments ($225,000 - $90,000) by $135,000 per year.

Accumulators primarily focus on building assets. Harvesters usually focus on deploying them. Stewards focus on preserving, building, deploying—and teaching others to do the same.

Stewards focus on preserving, building, deploying—and teaching others to do the same.

As we've seen so far, such complexities demand both a broader and deeper understanding of the economic landscape and the unique values and vision that drive your family's lifestyle choices and long-term goals. Therefore, it is important for the novice investor to know liabilities can represent debt as an interest bearing drag on income, or leverage as an income amplifier.

It is also important for new investors to know it is far more complicated than that. And, from the standpoint of generally accepted accounting practices (GAAP) and bank underwriting requirements, you can measure your balance sheet (assets and liabilities) debt-to-equity ratio, and many other indicators to determine whether your leverage is healthy or not. But you must start somewhere. Starting at an advanced level without a strong grasp of the basics can result in overemphasizing economic details, which may cause novices to disengage—or worse, to draw misguided conclusions or make decisions that undermine family values and connectedness.

The solution lies in adopting a stewardship investment philosophy and practical investment policy guidelines that reflect your family's values, vision, and goals.

The solution lies in adopting a stewardship investment philosophy and practical investment policy guidelines that reflect your family's values, vision, and goals—broad enough for all family members to understand and engage. Without meeting them where they are, family leaders risk alienating members who, with greater insight, might better appreciate the magnitude of the responsibility and grow into the roles they will one day assume.

San Diego, CA – March 15, 2006

Let's return to our Retail family. Prior to the recession, they had a net business income before taxes of $300,000[B] per month (milk). This is what their Portfolio Net Worth gameboard

---

[B] In 2006, $300,000 had purchasing power of approximately $477,000 in 2024.

THE RETAIL FAMILY
PORTFOLIO NET WORTH
DECEMBER 2006 (PRE-RECESSION)

	CLASS	INVESTED	USE	ALL ASSETS
ASSETS (+)	Securities/Cash	5,000,000		
	Businesses	11,000,000		
	Real Estate	23,000,000		
	Two Homes		2,900,000	
	Total	39,000,000	2,900,000	41,900,000
LIABILITIES (-)	Securities/Cash	0		
	Businesses	4,300,000		
	Real Estate	14,200,000		
	Two Homes		1,850,000	
	Total	18,500,000	1,850,000	20,350,000
RESULTS (+)	Net Worth	20,500,000	1,050,000	21,550,000

(cow) looked like at the time.

One important difference of the Portfolio Net Worth game-board, other than the sheer simplicity of it all for planning and presentation purposes, is the distinction between the use (consumption), marketable securities (liquid), real estate (illiquid with both moderate income and growth potential), and business (illiquid with high income and growth potential) categories.

The complexities and relentless dynamics of managing these basic categories amid the ups and downs of the various financial markets and the ebbs and flows of the economic environment are at the heart of why most family enterprises fail. Staying ahead of these issues requires constant attention. Living through them can also enhance the wisdom of all those who participate.

The gameboard provides family members with ballpark figures, before getting into the more detailed, and often complex, aspects of financial ratios mentioned earlier; these can be more meaningful when introduced to family members as they gain a better grasp of the big picture.

PLAYER OR SPECTATOR?

Author Israelmore Ayivor wisely said, "You are either a player or a spectator! Players influence the game, while spectators watch them do it. Such is life!"[2]

This mindset applies perfectly to managing family wealth. In family finances, being a player means actively engaging with the general numbers, understanding how assets work, and making informed decisions to influence outcomes. Spectators, on the other hand, simply watch the players move the wealth without ever fully participating in what is involved.

Being a player means actively engaging with the general numbers, understanding how assets work, and making informed decisions to influence outcomes.

Using the information presented on gameboards, a capable family member with interest and potential can take an active role, gaining insights that lead to actionable conclusions. Such a family member could see that the family's pretax return (milk) of $3.6 million per year on a $19.7 million invested asset (cow) yields an 18.3% return.

While this is clearly not aligned with GAAP, the gameboards have proved to be effective tools for providing context and clarity, and for facilitating communication and learning. However, it's important to recognize that, given human nature, there is always a risk. Sometimes, it doesn't take long for an uninformed family member or associate to jump to conclusions based on their understanding of what is in front of them. Therefore, it is critical for them to understand that, though they have a seat at the table as a player in training, it does not mean they have a vote until you, the family fiduciary, feel they are ready to do so and at what level.

OUTSIDE FORCES

The global environment and local and national circumstances and how they interact with your family's values, vision, and goals must all be factored into any decisions you make. The gameboards provide a framework, but it's the game-like dynamics and the attention they demand that introduce and foster interdependent interactions among family members. Each member brings his or her unique perspective, which is essential for meaningful participation in managing the family's wealth—its unique combination of love, wisdom, and money.

The gameboard is relatively useless when viewed in isolation. To truly play the game, it's vital to understand other factors that can influence the outcome, such as slow-moving economic trends, inflation, market cycles, or unexpected events, like the 9/11 attacks, market crashes, or pandemics. Between the retail family's Portfolio Net Worth gameboard in 2006 and 2024, the United States has experienced:[C]

- The Great Recession (2008);
- The longest economic recovery on record (2009–2020);
- The COVID-19 pandemic, which erased much of the

[C] Center on Budget and Policy Priorities, Macrotrends, and the U.S. Bureau of Labor Statistics.

recovery's gains (2020);

- Federal Reserve interest rate fluctuations: 4.09% in 2006, 0.05% in 2020, and 5.33% in 2024; and
- Inflation rising from 2.2% or lower in 2006 to 9.1% (the highest in 2022), now appearing to decline.

Without understanding how these events impacted your family's lifestyle cash flow and portfolio, they remain little more than uncontrollable news items, leaving you at their mercy. A perfect example of proactive planning is this family's response to the recession, which forced them to tap into their savings and reduce their lifestyle income by 40%.

Whether you play it or not, the family wealth game is relentless.

After the initial shock, and in the middle of it all, I asked the matriarch, "How are you holding up?" She surprised me with her answer: "Oh, we have been through this before. Our income has always been like waves on the ocean, up and down. I have gotten used to getting by spending under the swells when it's low and not overspending when it's rolling in."

What a great attitude!

It reminds me of a quote from Lou Holtz: "Nothing is as good as it seems, and nothing is as bad as it seems, but somewhere between reality falls."[3] This perspective is key when navigating the ups and downs of financial management. Managing family financial wealth requires a steady hand and a realistic outlook. There will be highs and lows, but the goal is to keep perspective. Neither success nor hardship lasts forever.

Whether you play it or not, the family wealth game is

relentless. You can ignore it. Leave it to chance or even play it casually. From what I can see, what works best is to proactively embrace the situation, engage the process, and work with what's available to make it through. It also helps if you can enjoy it as much as possible and get as many of those you love to join as a valuable family experience.

San Diego, CA – December 31, 2023

Among Warren Buffett's most famous strategies are five rules for building wealth: invest for the long-term, stay informed, maintain a competitive advantage, focus on quality, and manage risk.[4] It has been a winning strategy for him, but as we all know, it's easier said than done. So, what if you could make it a game? At the end of 2023, our retail family's Portfolio Net Worth gameboard looked something like this:

THE RETAIL FAMILY
PORTFOLIO NET WORTH
DECEMBER 2023

	CLASS	INVESTED	USE	ALL ASSETS
ASSETS (+)	Securities/Cash	18,700,000		
	Businesses	59,923,000		
	Real Estate	42,403,000		
	Four Homes		10,910,000	
	Total	121,026,000	10,910,000	131,936,000
LIABILITIES (–)	Securities/Cash	0		
	Businesses	12,300,000		
	Real Estate	10,626,000		
	Four Homes		3,764,000	
	Total	22,926,000	3,764,000	26,690,000
RESULTS (+)	Net Worth	98,100,000	7,146,000	105,246,000

Their strategy and execution have led to nearly fivefold

growth in invested assets over 17 years—despite enduring the five major events listed earlier and more than their share of personal family challenges. Of course, luck played a role as well, both good and bad. But their success did not just happen. The family was in the game the entire time and played to win. As family fiduciaries, they:

- Invested for the long-term, with a multigenerational time horizon;
- Stayed informed, updating their gameboards quarterly and checking the score;
- Maintained their competitive advantage—doing more of what was working and less of what was not;
- Focused on quality in relationships and investments, as well as a process with no short cuts; and,
- Managed risk with prudent leverage—setting realistic expectations and remaining flexible enough to adapt to change.

Like Ray Kroc said, "I was an overnight success all right, but thirty years is a long, long night."[5]

A SIMPLE GAME IN A COMPLEX WORLD

As we've discussed, money, as important as it is, might be the least important aspect of family wealth. Throughout this book, you've heard stories of various families, including mine, who have navigated all kinds of challenges. These families have committed to loving each other unconditionally and drawing on both inherited wisdom and life experiences, learning from their mistakes and successes along the way.

Love, wisdom, and money all matter, all the time. The stories in this book represent just a small sample of the countless issues, circumstances, and situations that arise within financially wealthy families. As a family fiduciary, you are responsible for managing these complexities in real time, often under less-than-ideal conditions. And you know no one can do it alone. Building and sustaining exceptional family wealth requires assistance from a range of specialists—people who deeply understand their area of expertise, know how to apply it practically, and can adapt it to your family's needs with compassion—and at a fair price.

> **Money, as important as it is, might be the least important aspect of family wealth.**

The best advisors aren't just doing a job—they're personally committed to delivering exceptional results. Doing a good job is expected, but those who go above and beyond are making a significant impact with both their expertise and the outcomes they help you achieve.

La Jolla, CA – September 7, 1987

Early in my career, I asked a colleague, "Do you know any good estate planning attorneys?" Little did I know, it was one of the luckiest days of my life. He said, "Yes, I'd like to introduce you to a friend of mine and a very good lawyer, Paul McEwen."

Paul was a kind and gentle man, tall in stature, friendly in nature, and extremely smart. Fifteen years my senior, he seemed to appreciate what I was trying to do. I liked him immediately. Over time we became the closest of friends. Along the way we began to work together. I would refer my clients to him for estate planning, and he would do the same for his clients who needed what he called "economic assistance." One day, after he introduced me to an extraordinary trust accountant, Jim Perich (another very lucky day), he explained, "When you get down to it, what the three of us do together is very simple to describe.

"Do you know what a milking stool looks like?" he asked.

I said, "A what?"

"You know, the small, three-legged stool an old-fashioned dairyman used to sit on to milk his cows."

Love, wisdom, and money all matter, all the time.

I pictured one immediately, and feeling kind of foolish, said "Oh, yes." He then pulled out his yellow legal pad and began to draw one. As he was drawing the three legs, he said, "Each one of us represents a leg of the stool. I am the legal-advice leg, Jim is the accounting- and tax-advice leg, and you are the economic-advice leg." And as he drew a circle representing the seat of the stool, he went on to say, "And the legs are held in place by the seat, the planning we do for our clients together."

His drawing made sense at the time, but I really did not understand the principles behind what he was describing.

"The stool only works properly when all three legs are balanced and tightly bonded," he said. "If one leg is shorter than the others or if the seat is loose, it's not going to function well." On that day, among other things, I learned the true meaning and value of professional collaboration. Paul, Jim, and I worked on many family wealth engagements together, including some mentioned in this book. While the fundamental principles of family wealth and legacy planning have remained the same, the complexities have grown significantly, requiring more intricate solutions.

In 2010, John A. Warnick, an estate planning attorney in Denver, with the help of Jay Hughes and others, founded the Purposeful Planning Institute (PPI). It's a nonprofit organization with a mission of "foster[ing] prosperous and purposeful relationships between professionals and their client families that endure multiple generations."[6] Today's version of the milking stool is also supported by a wide variety of planning collaborators. In addition to the traditional legal, accounting, and economic roles, collaborative advisory teams now include specialists in conflict resolution, philanthropic advising, wealth psychology, intergenerational communication, family services, substance abuse, aging services, and many others.

At PPI events, managing family wealth is about much more than just growing assets—it's about preserving the deeper values that hold a family together and preparing them to carry on, the very essence of generative wealth. The professionals at PPI understand that true wealth extends beyond the financial to the integration of love, wisdom, and money with purpose. As you collaborate with experts at this level, you realize that the most meaningful impact lies not only in accumulating financial capital, but in nurturing your family's legacy of values and intergenerational continuity.

Legacy is not simply about the financial wealth you leave behind. Your legacy is the direct result of the individual decisions you make each day of your life and how the results are viewed by others. It is about the values, memories, and wisdom you impart, and the impact it has on those you love. And whether you actively plan for it or not, that will be your legacy.

Even if you spend all your money, squander your love and wisdom, have no children, leave it all to charity, or any combination of these choices, your legacy will ultimately be determined by the life you led and the impact you had on others.

By now I hope you realize you are already deep into your own Legacy Estate game. So, if you are interested, let's see what you might do about it, if anything, in the next chapter.

8

THE LEGACY ESTATE GAME

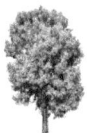

"You can't teach a kid to ride a bike at a seminar."

DAVID SANDLER

Who are you? And what do you want?

By truthfully answering these questions, your family's love and wisdom fuse together to form your family's values. These are the guidelines by which you make decisions and run your life. Only with careful attention and foresight can you and your family crystallize a vision for the future. This vision will guide you in creating a practical, step-by-step action plan (goals) that will lead your family interdependently toward the future you want to achieve. The way you live your life today, and every day, is through your love and wisdom—and your money in action. It is the legacy you are actively creating—one that will be felt by those who know you now, as well as by future generations who will hear about your actions and draw their own conclusions.

The financial assets and resources you pass on during your life or after you're gone, often considered the core of one's legacy, are simply tools for the next generation to chart their own path. While they will make their own choices, the values and vision you demonstrated in how you lived day to day will deeply influence their decisions and direction. In *Borrowed from Your Grandchildren* Dennis Jaffe reveals how you can learn from families who have done things in a way to sustain and expand their fortunes across

> *As your legacy estate plan unfolds, you are preparing your end game strategy.*

generations. Specifically, he highlights how "generative families" achieve more than just greater financial wealth; they create great families. As he puts it, "These special families are also successful in the development of future generations and expressing their values in everything they do."[1]

ESTATE PLANNING: END GAME OR A NEW BEGINNING?

Why not settle your estate while you are alive? This way you can see what happens and fix it if you do not like what you see. It makes sense, but few families do it. And though it sounds odd, that is just what a client, the chief financial officer of a privately held real estate conglomerate, asked us to do. He said, "I would like you to have a meeting with my wife as though I had passed away a month before, just for me to get a feel for what she would be going through if it happened."

"What a loving thing to do," I said. "That's a good idea. No one has ever asked us to do that before." After thinking about it a bit, I said, "There's just one rule."

"What's that?"

I responded, "You can't talk during the meeting."

"Why not?"

"Because you'll be dead."

It was a great meeting. He watched as she made decisions he may not have agreed with and would probably never make. As she did, it was all he could do, including biting his lower lip, to keep from talking. We all learned a lot that day. And today, with some additional hard-earned insight, their legacy estate plan is the better for it.

As your legacy estate plan unfolds, you are preparing your end game strategy. It's sort of like the fourth quarter in football, the ninth inning in baseball, or late in the last period in many other sports. As in most athletic competitions, tomorrow there will be today's game film for the players and coaches to review and revise their game plan. For those who play the next game, it will be available to glean some wisdom from and build upon.

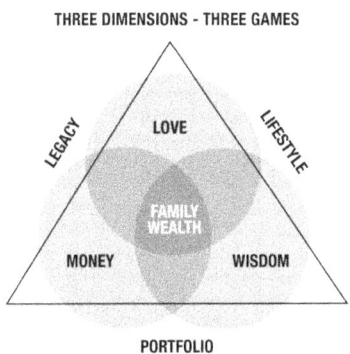

Instead of being viewed as the final step, your legacy estate plan can serve as a bridge, using the current "chapter" of your family's story (the game film) to lay the foundation for the next phase of your family wealth strategy.

San Diego, CA – December 20, 2017

After recovering from the Great Recession and flourishing once again, our retail family faced new challenges just two years before the outbreak of the COVID-19 pandemic. With their eldest child now in his thirties, the patriarch and matriarch had two pressing questions:

- What can we do to prepare our children to handle all they will be inheriting?
- What about estate taxes?

Their concerns were valid. The children were not ready, and the estate taxes would be in the tens of millions of dollars. So, they set two goals: (1) Prepare the next generation to handle their family wealth the best they could, and (2) Legally avoid as much estate tax as possible.

A VOLUNTARY TAX?

In 1977, George Cooper, a Columbia University law professor, in his words, "trained in the arcane act of estate law practice," and under the auspices of the Studies of Government Finance: Second Series, posed the question and published the article "A Voluntary Tax? New Perspectives on Sophisticated Estate Tax Avoidance" in the *Columbia Law Review*.

In 1974, President Gerald Ford signed into law the Employee Retirement Income Security Act (ERISA) setting new standards of conduct for fiduciaries. In 1976, he signed the Tax Reform Act (TRA), at which time Professor Cooper stated that this law "… only changes the rules of the avoidance game."

In response to what many considered these somewhat game-changing laws, in 1979, the storied Brookings Institution, an independent organization devoted to non-partisan research, education, and publication in economics, government as well as the social sciences, republished Professor Cooper's article in book form.

> *"There are two systems of taxation in our country: one for the informed and one for the uninformed."*

In my many years of experience working with estate planning and tax attorneys, as well as their IRS counterparts, I have observed that the fundamental principles of both ERISA and TRA have remained largely unchanged, aside from adjustments to exclusion, exemption, and deduction categories and amounts. For example, at the time of this writing, the individual estate tax exemption is $13.61 million. However, this amount is scheduled to decrease to approximately $7 million on December 31, 2025, unless extended by the current administration. While the tax rate itself is not set to change, the reduction in the exemption amount could significantly impact planning strategies. By the time you read this, the outcome will likely be known.

Regardless, the principle that citizens have the right to minimize their taxes within the bounds of the law is well captured in two quotes by the esteemed Learned Hand, U.S. federal judge, lawyer, and judicial philosopher:

- "There are two systems of taxation in our country: one for the informed and one for the uninformed."[2]
- "Any one may so arrange his affairs that his taxes shall be as low as possible; he is not bound to choose that pattern which will best pay the Treasury."[3]

TWO GOALS, ONE LEGACY ESTATE GAME

Fortunately, our retail family has already begun laying the groundwork, gradually transferring their family's wealth of love and wisdom as part of their seventh-generation legacy, along with a portion of their financial wealth, to their heirs in waiting.

This approach ensured that their estate planning would remain relevant and responsive to any unforeseen changes.

Long before the recession, as an act of foresight and love, the parents set up individual property trusts for each of their children. These legal instruments allowed them to transfer small amounts of assets, giving the children the opportunity to manage these holdings. More importantly, this strategy also served the critical purpose of freezing the value of these appreciating assets at the time of the gift, legally and effectively reducing the parents' taxable estate and transferring the assets at least one, and in some cases, two generations into the future.

Though a good start, the parents' financial assets were growing like a snowball rolling downhill. They felt the time had come to develop an even longer-term, more robust family asset transfer strategy. In 2017, relatively early in their Legacy Estate game, their gameboard looked like the one on the next page.

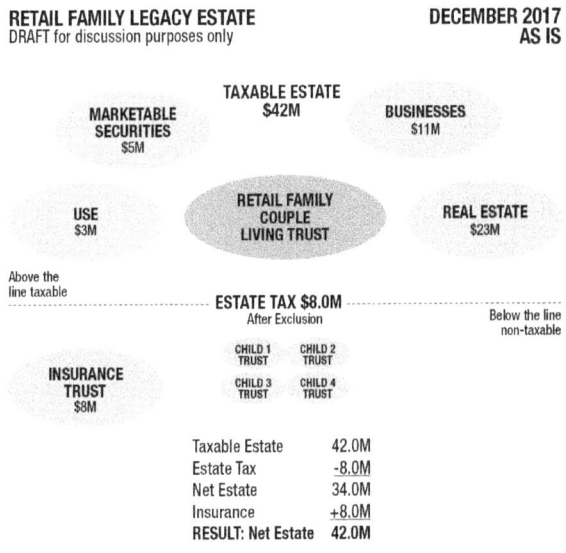

RETAIL FAMILY LEGACY ESTATE
DRAFT for discussion purposes only

DECEMBER 2017
AS IS

TAXABLE ESTATE
$42M

MARKETABLE
SECURITIES
$5M

BUSINESSES
$11M

USE
$3M

RETAIL FAMILY
COUPLE
LIVING TRUST

REAL ESTATE
$23M

Above the
line taxable

ESTATE TAX $8.0M
After Exclusion

Below the line
non-taxable

INSURANCE
TRUST
$8M

CHILD 1
TRUST

CHILD 2
TRUST

CHILD 3
TRUST

CHILD 4
TRUST

Taxable Estate	42.0M
Estate Tax	-8.0M
Net Estate	34.0M
Insurance	+8.0M
RESULT: Net Estate	42.0M

The Legacy Estate gameboard, like the other gameboards, is divided into top, bottom, and results sections. The key difference in the Legacy Estate gameboard is that it visually separates assets by titles, including trusts. The assets shown "above the line" are part of the current fiduciary generation's taxable estate, while those "below the line" are not included in the parents' estate and therefore not subject to the estate tax.

The results section, as with the other gameboards, is a summary comparing the holdings above and below the line. This allows the family to consider various proposed scenarios. For example, the gameboard above represents the estate tax estimation as of December 2017. At that point in time, given the family's prior decisions and experiences, they held a meeting with all family members. Their goal was to evaluate a more tax-efficient scenario for their Legacy Estate game, and their agenda looked like this:

AGENDA

Opening Remarks – Retail Couple
- Purpose
- Goals

Game Overview – Advisor
- Big Picture Context
- Progress to Date
- Strategy Forward
- Phases
- Update/Reviews

Game Plan – Planner
- Current Situation
- Proposed Next Phase
- Action Items

Discussion – All
- Questions
- Concerns
- Resolution

Closing Remarks – Retail Couple

During the meeting, the family decided to approach both goals incrementally. They felt most comfortable with a phased strategy—one that was flexible enough to implement their current scenario as if it were final, while remaining adaptable for future adjustments as life circumstances evolved. This approach ensured that their estate planning would remain relevant and responsive to any unforeseen changes, providing both peace of mind and the ability to reassess when necessary.

Below is what the proposed scenario at the time looked like:

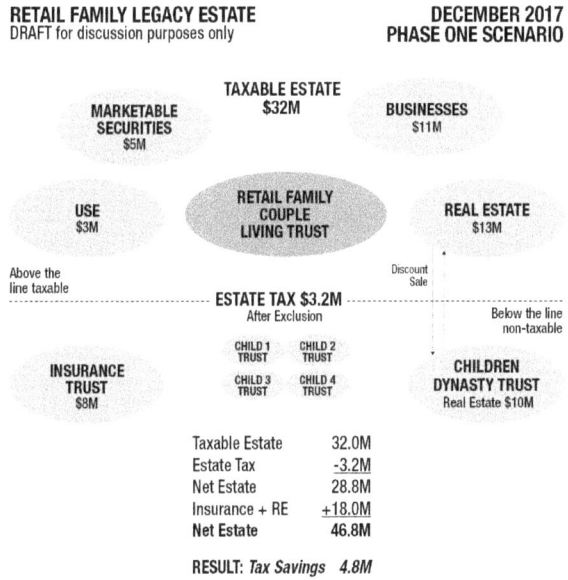

RETAIL FAMILY LEGACY ESTATE
DRAFT for discussion purposes only

DECEMBER 2017
PHASE ONE SCENARIO

TAXABLE ESTATE
$32M

MARKETABLE
SECURITIES
$5M

BUSINESSES
$11M

USE
$3M

RETAIL FAMILY
COUPLE
LIVING TRUST

REAL ESTATE
$13M

Above the
line taxable

Discount
Sale

ESTATE TAX $3.2M
After Exclusion

Below the line
non-taxable

INSURANCE
TRUST
$8M

CHILD 1
TRUST

CHILD 2
TRUST

CHILD 3
TRUST

CHILD 4
TRUST

CHILDREN
DYNASTY TRUST
Real Estate $10M

Taxable Estate	32.0M
Estate Tax	-3.2M
Net Estate	28.8M
Insurance + RE	+18.0M
Net Estate	46.8M

RESULT: *Tax Savings 4.8M*

The primary action item of the proposed scenario strategy was for the parents to sell a minority interest in their commercial real estate business to a generation-skipping trust (commonly referred to as a dynasty trust) in exchange for a note. This note would be paid for over several years with income from the real estate, with the goal of completing the payments before the end of the parents' expected lifespans. The sale was discounted to reflect the lack of control and non-marketability of the minority interest.

The three goals at this point were to transfer some assets to the next generation, educate the children on how to manage their future inheritance, and position the family to reduce a portion of their estate tax liability. While the strategy was based on certain assumptions and not guaranteed to succeed as planned, its implementation not only transferred a portion of the wealth and educated the children on managing intergenerational financial assets but also increased the likelihood of significantly reducing future estate tax liabilities.

It's important to note that legacy estate planning is never truly over. It is an ongoing process, shaped by evolving family dynamics and financial circumstances. At any given time, the best scenario solution is influenced by what is happening within the family and what makes sense in their current financial situation. Each new phase of life requires a fresh look at the estate plan, adapting it to new realities and continuing to seek optimal solutions.

ABOVE THE LINE/ BELOW THE LINE GAME PLAN

Prior to implementing the proposed scenario, the family's December 2017 "Current Situation" was a typical parent-generation strategy of controlling all aspects of the family financial wealth with very little, if any, involvement of the next generation.

Upon implementation of the scenario, the game provided the medium for the children to experience the methodical process of learning how the wealth transfer process works and how to manage their own separate property trusts. This game allowed them to begin to get a feel for the benefits of both a "below the line" irrevocable life insurance trust (ILIT) and generation-skipping tax trust (GST). As the entire family became more involved in the game and adept at the process, they also became more prepared for whatever was to come.

As we learned in the previous chapter, the retail family's financial fortune has continued to grow. The next generation's ability to enrich the family's wealth—not just its finances, but also its love and wisdom—has expanded significantly. Today, they are not only taking greater responsibility for managing the family's wealth but are also more capable of handling their personal assets. They are better prepared than ever to inherit the family legacy and, in turn, pass along the values of love, wisdom, and money to future generations.

> *[Legacy estate planning] is an ongoing process, shaped by evolving family dynamics and financial circumstances.*

By working through the retail and other families' Cash Flow, Portfolio, and Legacy Estate gameboards, you have been exposed to a sense of the power behind the process and discipline required for a successful family wealth enrichment plan.

This approach demands active involvement from family members and a growing awareness of both the big-picture strategy and the details that each participant brings to the table—whether they are heirs, attorneys, accountants, economic advisors, planners, or other full- and part-time contributors. Together, these efforts are essential to nurture, protect, and grow your family's wealth.

EVERYONE'S FAVORITE CHANNEL: WIIFM

"What's in it, for me?"

According to Northern Trust, the 135-year-old administration financial institution that currently has $16.5 trillion assets under custody, there are three primary individual family member concerns regarding intergenerational wealth transfer: the participants' self-determination, their individual competence, and their need for autonomy in relatedness.[4]

In other words, everybody wants to win from their point of view.

Beyond fulfilling individual psychological needs and the potential confidence and joy of winning, participating in the family wealth game offers added benefits: fostering familial interaction, promoting fun and learning, stimulating the mind, and providing participants with a sense of influence and the opportunity to contribute to building a brighter and more impactful family wealth legacy.

Everybody wants to win from their point of view.

But there is no such thing as a game without rules.

The complexity of today's games—particularly one as meaningful as the family wealth game—calls for rules, and a gamemaster. In multiplayer games, a gamemaster is defined as the organizer who ensures the rules are followed, acts as an arbitrator or moderator, and facilitates gameplay. This role is even more common and valuable in collaborative games, where teamwork is emphasized, rather than in competitive settings.

The gamemaster role is also to facilitate weaving the other participant game-player stories and goals together, control the non-player aspects of the game, create an environment where players can interact, and assist in solving player disputes.

The fundamental function of the gamemaster is the same

for all interactive games, with differing circumstances and outcome priorities dictating the duties of the gamemaster unique to that unique system.

Though they may be called gamemasters today, when it comes to the central oversight and administration support of family wealth, there has been another name these third-party facilitators have been called for centuries: the family office.

To see the parallels and what this could mean to you and your family, you may want to dive into the next chapter to see inside the modern virtual family office of today.

9

THE MODERN FAMILY OFFICE GAMEMASTER

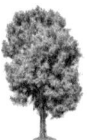

*"You do not rise to the level of your goals.
You fall to the level of your systems."*

JAMES CLEAR

By now it is evident that healthy, sustainable family wealth—encompassing love, wisdom, and money—doesn't happen by chance. One of the core messages of this book is that family wealth, aligned with your family's values and vision for the future, must be intentionally built and nurtured to thrive over time; it requires ongoing effort to develop, implement, measure, analyze, adapt, reevaluate, and continuously reimagine.

To support this idea, families with significant financial wealth looking to establish a centralized oversight and administration entity, often turn to the family office model. While today's family offices may share certain similarities to family offices of old formerly only affordable to the ultrarich, each one is now unique in its own way—leading to the saying "If you have seen one family office … you have seen one family office." There is and never has been a formal standard defining what a family office is or does; typically, its structure and effectiveness reflect the functionality—and dysfunctionality—of the family it serves.

Yet, if you look deeper, the core purpose of most family offices remains the same: to protect and grow the family's financial wealth for both the present and future. When it comes to addressing the love and wisdom aspects of family wealth, the approach taken by one family office over another is often inconsistent to say the least. While some family offices do consider the people side of family wealth, many just tend the money. And even among those sensitive to the matter, the level of focus and attention given varies significantly from one office to another.

This chapter is dedicated to what we have learned in working directly with those families committed to attending to and building upon all three: love, wisdom, and money. Today's technology makes it much easier, more robust, and more manageable than ever.

In the past, families were required to either staff and house their own single family office, join another family's family office, or outsource the duties to a commercial entity or bank family office, as described in one of the many Russ Alan Prince and Hannah Shaw Grove books on the subject.[1]

OUT WITH THE OLD AND IN WITH THE NEW

With the significant holdings now controlled by households in the 90th to 99.9th percentiles, the need for family office-style organization, clarity, and efficiency has grown substantially. It is both feasible and economically sensible to centrally oversee and integrate a family's love, wisdom, money, values, vision, goals, and advisory team into a cohesive ecosystem. This can be achieved through available processes and technology, aligned with the principles of the Lifestyle, Portfolio, and Legacy games, all under the framework of a virtual family office.

"If you have seen one family office ... you have seen one family office."

This is possible because many families who have achieved or are approaching this level of significant financial wealth—and who benefit from a family office—already have much of the necessary structure in place, thanks to prior planning and established personal and professional relationships. Your family may be one of them.

If so, from your current position of strength and relationships, and by adopting a comprehensive strategic approach like the ones illustrated, you are only a few steps away from one unified, sustainable, and continuously improving generative effort.

BACK TO THE FUTURE

In chapter five, you were introduced to a real-world example of a virtual family office in action. This example featured an entrepreneurial spouse in her eighties who became the family fiduciary steward after her husband's stroke left her managing their complex fortune. Her husband had put the necessary components in place but managed them reactively, addressing issues as they arose—a common scenario among rugged individualist entrepreneurs. While he had a vision, his approach remained largely break-fix, doing what he felt was necessary at the time.

In contrast, his wife did not share these tendencies or aspirations, and instead reached out to a trusted individual, her estate planning attorney, to help her gain perspective and control over the monumental task she faced.

The following graphic illustrates a typical progression through the different levels of family wealth planning, framed by the principles of love, wisdom, and money.

When we first met, I introduced her to the family wealth game and Lifestyle, Portfolio, and Legacy gameboards. Her response was simply, "That's it?"

With that glimpse of her big picture, she naturally adopted a virtual family office view of her family fiduciary responsibilities. And, eventually, her successor trustee son would do the same.

Today, he is teaching his most engaged son and other adult children to become proficient in utilizing the same perspective, approach, and system, ensuring a consistent generative strategy for them to build upon and pass along.

When his mother passed away, only a short time after he became the successor trustee of his father's trust, he confided in us that he didn't feel equipped to settle her estate and manage the family wealth. A few years later, looking back, he said, "Sometimes you think you are in trouble, when it actually works out for the best." His sentiment underscores the benefit of having a virtual family office structure, a system that not only provides the necessary support and continuity during difficult transitions, but also empowers family members to adapt, learn, and ultimately grow from challenging experiences.

"Sometimes you think you are in trouble, when it actually works out for the best."

There are plenty of planning systems and experts available to help you establish your own virtual family office to integrate your family wealth—love, wisdom, money—trifecta. If you choose to do so, your most important plan of action is:

First, adopt a big-picture and comprehensive open-ended perspective—no one ever really knows what is going to happen next.

Second, embrace a structure that feels right for you, knowing there are distinct categories that will relentlessly call for your attention—Lifestyle, Portfolio, and Legacy—when making major decisions.

Third, with a unified model for oversight and trusted advisors for specialized guidance, you can effectively plan, coordinate, and manage every aspect to reach your desired goals.

THE MANY ROLES OF A FAMILY OFFICE

In the previous pages, we introduced a variety of roles that your family office can fulfill—twenty-two in all. Through some of the stories, you've seen the value of centralized oversight and administration, enterprise continuity, family and advisory team governance, internal and external communication, planning, implementation, wealth transfer, tax reduction, and asset protection.

While there may be more roles yet to be discovered, some additional ones include providing a forum for "master mind" exercises and collaboration, facilitating conflict resolution, engaging in philanthropic outreach, acting as a family historian, setting investment policy, performing due diligence and risk management, negotiating on behalf of the family, and even becoming a profit center when the savings from family office strategies exceed operational costs.

But there is one more major role of a family office, which is worthy of another quick story or two.

Campbell, OH – October 1, 1964

I was first introduced to what I later recognized as my family's "family bank" shortly after I graduated from high school, got a job, and wanted to buy a car. Without resources of my own and no credit rating, I turned to my father, the blue-collar entrepreneur who always spent less than he earned and saved the rest. I asked if he could help me as he had helped my older brother four years earlier.

He said, "I can't just give you the money."

I said, "Why not?"

He responded, "I loaned money to your brother to buy his car. He has been paying me back. But if I had given it outright to him, I wouldn't have anything to loan to you now."

Being a quick study and one who could never keep his mouth shut, I said, "Oh, I get it. And if you just give it to me, you won't have it to lend to my younger brothers when they need it." He went on to say something about how I had a "keen grasp for the obvious" and loaned me the money.

Our family bank was a small black ledger book. In it, my dad had a section for each of his sons. When he made a loan, he entered the amount and the date. He also entered each payment made. He kept a running total until each of us eventually paid him off in full. It was simple and clear, held us each accountable, and spoke volumes about how he and my mother valued money and the proper way to use it.

Palm Springs, CA – October 16, 2007

Years later I worked with another family whose family's bank operated on a much grander scale. When the surviving spouse passed away, the family bank held assets of around $18 million. According to the estate plan, a significant portion of these assets was placed in trust to provide lifetime income for their adult children, with the corpus of it eventually passing to each child's descendants upon their death.

Much like my father's approach, this family bank also offered market-rate loans to family members who couldn't otherwise qualify for traditional financing. These loans supported everything from home purchases to business ventures and debt refinancing. However, unlike my father's informal black journal, a family bank of this size—with an ever-growing number of borrowers and lenders across generations—required a robust set of formal rules to ensure its long-term viability. James Hughes offers the following insightful guidelines on the workings of family banks across generations:[2]

> *The family bank can play a key role in guiding everyone on their individual wealth journeys and fostering a healthy pursuit of happiness.*

- **View family bank as informal.** While not a formal institution, its informality preserves privacy and allows it to evolve as the family evolves.

- **Set up formal rules and meetings.** Despite its informality, a family bank should have officers, directors, and advisors, as well as established procedures for processing and servicing loans.

- **Incorporate family values in the mission.** The family bank's mission statement should reflect the family's philosophy, purpose, policies, and consequences in case of default.

- **Select capable trustees.** Trustees of family trust play a critical role in both the family bank and overall governance, requiring careful selection with clear parameters set forth.

- **Mission statement agreement.** All participating family members must agree with the mission statement, like any borrower-lender relationship.
- **Maintain accurate and timely accounting.** Every participating member should receive clear information on the terms of the agreements and the status of each.

LOVE, WISDOM, MONEY FULL CIRCLE

In the context of holistic family wealth, the family bank is more than just a financial institution—it acts as a central hub for your family's love, wisdom, and money. It brings these elements together, embodying your family's values and vision. By supporting each family member's Lifestyle, Portfolio, and Legacy, the family bank can play a key role in guiding everyone on their individual wealth journeys and fostering a healthy pursuit of happiness.

No matter where you and your family are on your life journey today, your dedication to enriching all aspects of your family wealth truly matters.

In its most basic form, the family bank's purpose is to assist a family member or members as they strive to maximize their individual and collective love and wisdom—their human potential. It also can serve to enhance the continuity of the family enterprise as a sustainable, multigenerational, and potentially generative enterprise.

Participating in the operations, meetings, and mutual

accountabilities of the family bank enriches relationships and deepens understanding among family members, enhancing their love for one another and the family. The formality of these activities helps each member to better recognize fundamental principles of human intelligence in action. Participating in the process builds upon the sound judgment within the family banking rules, which are grounded in and reinforce the family's values and intellectual capital, ultimately contributing to its collective wisdom.

All of this, combined with the ability to leverage family resources for endeavors aligned with the family's love, wisdom, and vision, can lead to meaningful economic gains—using money as the practical tool it is.

Nearly every family has some version of a family bank. Yours, whether basic or highly developed, has the potential to become a keystone for your family's future prosperity.

No matter where you and your family are on your life journey today—whatever your current family values, love, wisdom, financial resources, and vision may be—your dedication to enriching all aspects of your family wealth truly matters.

Embracing this commitment has the potential to become the most impactful endeavor of your life and those you love.

10

GAME ON!

"To know and not do, is to not yet know."

ATTRIBUTED TO CONFUCIUS

I thought you said it was simple!"

Most people's head spin with all the talk about love, wisdom, money, lifestyle, portfolio, legacy, values, vision, goals, family dynamics, family offices, family banks, advisory teams, and generative intergenerational family wealth. It doesn't have to send you into a spiral, though. If one picture is worth a thousand words, how about two pictures? The first depicts what is likely to happen to your family wealth without a path and plan. (See next page.)

The second gives you an idea of what could happen when you set your family up to carry on. (See page 136.)

By simplifying the complexities and creating a thoughtful plan, you can guide your family toward a future of purpose and unity. If I have done what I set out to do writing this book, the big picture of who you are and what you want for your family will include a larger landscape than when you began reading. If not, that's on me. As it was at the outset, the outcome of your

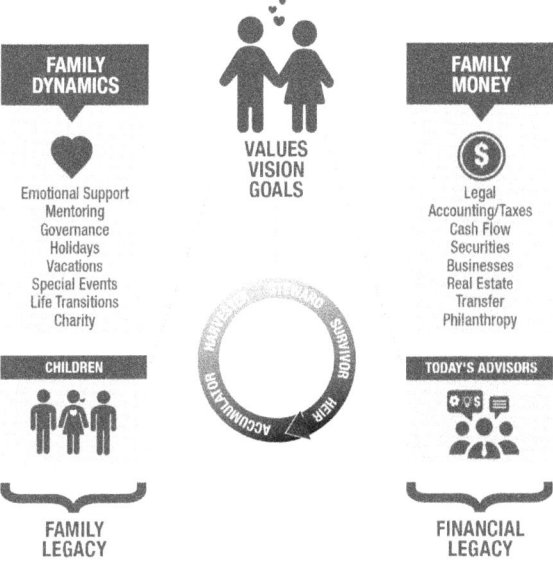

family's future depends on your actions and the systems you, as your family fiduciary steward, put in place from here on out. It's up to you to do what you can to proactively protect, engage, lead, and envision what your family might become. Just one more story.

Houston, TX – November 2, 2014

On a beautiful fall morning, a matriarch we had worked with for over 25 years felt cautiously optimistic about going to brunch with her son and his wife. Their relationship had been strained over the past year, as nearly every decision she made was met with criticism from them. I knew her as an intelligent, considerate, and loving mother who had done extensive estate planning and gifting on behalf of her family. She was always mindful of equitable attention and distribution to her children

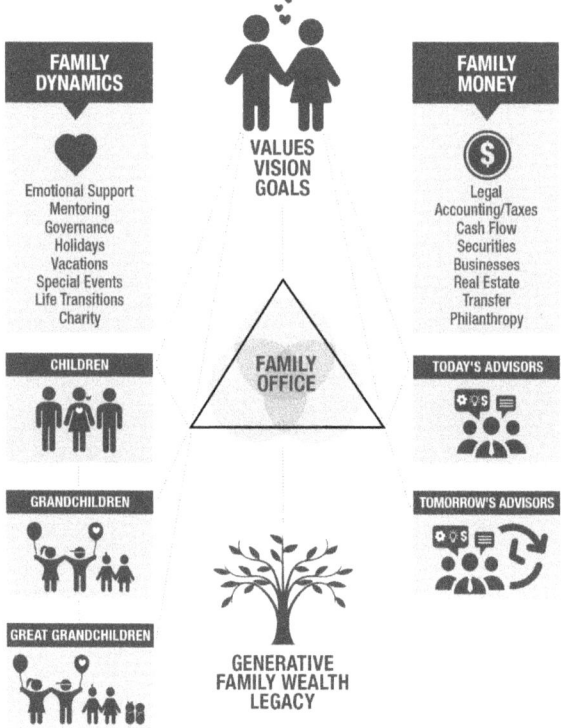

and was interested in preparing them to carry on their family values.

Throughout our time working together, she had maintained healthy relationships with her other adult children and all her grandchildren, making the recent tension with this couple particularly puzzling. But today felt different. For the past few weeks, their interactions were cordial, with a new sense of ease and understanding. When they invited her to one of the city's most elegant restaurants—a place so popular it required reservations weeks in advance—she hoped it was a sign of a fresh start. As they sat at their table, they appeared as healthy and happy as any intergenerational family could. But the facade soon cracked. The couple began to provoke her, referencing recent decisions and condemning her cognitive abilities.

This was a woman in her late eighties who, from everything I knew, was as sharp as ever. She had a Ph.D. and had built a family fortune on her own while caring for a husband who was injured in a household accident 20 years earlier. She had moved to the area to be closer to her children. With their future in mind, she purchased a ranch and developed enough land for each child to build a home if they wished. Initially, all three children and their families were excited about the possibilities.

As your family fiduciary, part of your role is to act as an agent of gradual and successful change, especially when faced with unforeseen circumstances.

But the couple at brunch today had other ideas.

They accused her of being mentally incompetent, saying things like, "You must be crazy thinking you can develop a ranch." "You're being frivolous, unorganized, taken advantage of, and wasting money." "You don't have any idea what you're doing. It's a disaster."

They were relentless. To a bystander, the conversation might have looked normal, but it was an all-out submarine-like attack. Blindsided, she didn't know how to react at first. She soon realized they must have been intentionally provoking her to make a scene in a public place. After several minutes of relentless jabs, though hurt and angry on the inside, she managed to keep her composure. She then stood, calmly, and politely excused herself—and walked out. A few days later when she described the scene to me, she said, "In the moment, it was all I could do to refrain myself from lashing out in self-defense, until it hit me, that was exactly what they wanted. They set me up."

She then said, "When I got in the car, I had a difficult time processing what happened. The feeling of joy from reuniting with them was overcome by feelings of betrayal and sorrow that my own child and his wife would turn on me in such a way."

The best approach is to focus on the present situation and how you choose to navigate it.

She eventually discovered that this was not the first time they had done such a thing. She told me, "I came to find out earlier that year there was a similar event with my daughter-in-law's aging mother. A scene in a public place, followed by more accusations questioning her decision-making abilities, until they eventually had her officially deemed incompetent."

The daughter-in-law then gained power of attorney over her widowed mother's significant assets. She isolated her siblings from anything to do with their mother's money, and, despite their opposition, remained in control and somehow justified whatever she did with it.

It appeared to be what I call "a money grab," or in this case a kind of elder abuse extortion. The couple must have felt emboldened by the way it worked out for them before—and determined to try it again. Apparently for them, there was no thought of love. They probably thought they were smart, but they obviously were not wise. They made it all about the money.

Fortunately, our matriarch was able to avoid what could have been a disaster and successfully protected her dignity, legacy, and family wealth.

FAMILY FIDUCIARIES IN ACTION

In the words of World War II veteran, English professor, and poet A.R. Ammons, "Clarity, order, meaning, structure, rationality: they are necessary to whatever provisional stability we have, and they can be the agents of gradual and successful change."[1]

As your family fiduciary, part of your role is to act as an agent of gradual and successful change, especially when faced with unforeseen circumstances. None of the families mentioned in this book knew what was around the corner. Whether it was the good fortune of windfalls or business success, or the support or alienation of their children, some navigated these challenges successfully and prevailed, while others struggled.

Throughout these stories, the principles of clarity, order, meaning, and structure consistently emerge. Whether it's the steady stewardship of the San Diego retail family, the resilience of a family rebuilding after 9/11, or the strength of a Tijuana family facing poverty, each narrative highlights unique challenges along the family wealth continuum. Stories of forgiveness for deeply troubled loved ones, the journeys of ancestors navigating citizenship or immigration, and the experiences of surviving spouses, trustees, spendthrifts, and hoarders all reflect a shared, uncertain path—filled with dangers, opportunities, and profound lessons.

As a family fiduciary steward, it's essential to recognize that everyone inherently acts out of self-interest—yourself, your family members, and all of us—before, if ever, considering the broader family wealth picture. The best approach is to focus on the present situation and how you choose to navigate it. With the help and support of trustworthy family members and advisors, you can plan and act intentionally to prosper, monitor results, assess progress, refocus on priorities, and repeat the process continuously for the benefit of everyone involved.

Houston, TX – January 29, 2015

After our matriarch above recovered from the emotional events she experienced, though very much still brokenhearted, she felt compelled to do something to fulfill her family fiduciary steward responsibilities.

She came to me with a plan. "I've decided to amend my trust," she said. "I'm going to reallocate a portion of what I originally intended to leave to my son to a charity. It will benefit at-risk children ages 5 to 18, where everyone in their community understands the importance of healthy loving relationships." This action was more than a financial decision; it was a testament to what mattered most to her.

> *This action was more than a financial decision; it was a testament to what mattered most to her.*

What matters most to you? I've come to realize that all any of us really have is today. And what we do today, and every day, will ultimately become our legacies. As Confucius is attributed as saying, "We have two lives, and the second begins when we realize we only have one." This is your life: your family wealth, your journey, your treasure hunt, your opportunity, your love, your wisdom, your money, your lifestyle, your portfolio, your legacy.

The question now is this: Where do you want to take it from here?

All the best to you and yours to make it all it can be.

Notes

Introduction

1 Adam Hayes, "Dotcom Bubble Definition," Investopedia, updated May 31, 2024, https://www.investopedia.com/terms/d/dotcom-bubble.asp.

2 See Dan Sullivan, *The Laws of Lifetime Growth: Always Make Your Future Bigger Than Your Past* (Berrett-Koehler, 2006).

Chapter 1

1 David R. York, *The Gift of Lift: Harnessing the Power of Stewardship to Elevate the World* (Köehler Books, 2022).

Chapter 2

1 C.S. Lewis, *The Four Loves* (HarperOne, 2017).

2 See 1 Corinthians 13:7.

3 James E. Hughes Jr., *Family: The Compact Among Generations* (Bloomberg Press, 2007); James E. Hughes, Jr. (website), accessed December 31, 2024, https://www.jamesehughes.com/about.

4 Stephen R. Covey, *The 7 Habits of Highly Effective People: Powerful Lessons in Personal Change* (Free Press, 1989).

Chapter 3

1 John Kenneth Galbraith, *The Affluent Society* (Boston: Houghton Mifflin, 1958). Galbraith introduced the idea of balancing economic security with entrepreneurial risk-taking, suggesting that these two forces can synergize to foster both stability and growth in society.

2 Viktor E. Frankl, *Man's Search for Meaning* (Beacon Press, 2006).

Chapter 4

1 *Jerry Maguire*, directed by Cameron Crowe (TriStar Pictures, 1996).

2 James E. Hughes Jr., *Family Wealth—Keeping It in the Family: How Family Members and Their Advisers Preserve Human, Intellectual, and*

Financial Assets for Generations, rev. ed. (Bloomberg Press, 2004).

3 Often attributed to George Bernard Shaw and Mark Twain.

4 Yuval Noah Harari, *Sapiens: A Brief History of Humankind* (Harper, 2015).

Chapter 5

1 For the full parable, visit "The Blind Men and the Elephant," Peace Corps, https://www.peacecorps.gov/educators-and-students/educators/resources/blind-men-and-elephant/story-blind-men-and-elephant/.

Chapter 6

1 Tom Vander Ark, "8 Principles of Productive Gamification," Getting Smart, February 20, 2014, https://www.gettingsmart.com/2014/02/20/8-principles-productive-gamification/; Misho Zghuladze, "8 Core Principles of Gamification or 'How to Gamify Anything,'" *Forbes*, November 27, 2023, https://forbes.ge/en/8-core-principles-of-gamification-or-how-to-gamify-anything/.

2 Jane McGonigal, *SuperBetter: A Revolutionary Approach to Getting Stronger, Happier, Braver, and More Resilient* (Penguin Press, 2015).

3 Robert T. Kiyosaki, *Rich Dad Poor Dad: What the Rich Teach Their Kids About Money—That the Poor and Middle Class Do Not!* (Plata Publishing, 1997).

4 Stephen R. Covey, A. Roger Merrill, and Rebecca R. Merrill, *First Things First* (Free Press, 1994).

5 Dave Ramsey, *The Legacy Journey: A Radical View of Biblical Wealth and Generosity* (Ramsey Press, 2014).

Chapter 7

1 James Royal, "Are You Rich Enough to Be in the Top 1%? Here's How Much Income and Wealth It Takes," Bankrate.com, published November 29, 2024, https://www.bankrate.com/investing/income-wealth-top-1-percent/.

2 Israelmore Ayivor, *The Great Hand Book of Quotes* (CreateSpace, 2014).

3 Lou Holtz, *Wins, Losses, and Lessons: An Autobiography* (HarperCollins, 2006).

4   Daniel Shvartsman, "Warren Buffett's Investment Strategy, Investing Rules, and How He Made His Fortune," Investing.com, updated October 16, 2024, https://www.investing.com/academy/trading/warren-buffett-investment-strategy-rules-fortune/.

5   Ray Kroc, with Robert Anderson, *Grinding It Out: The Making of McDonald's* (St. Martin's Paperbacks, 1987).

6   "About Us," Purposeful Planning Institute, accessed January 4, 2025, https://purposefulplanninginstitute.com/about-us/.

Chapter 8

1   Dennis T. Jaffe, *Borrowed from Your Grandchildren: The Evolution of 100-Year Family Enterprises* (Wiley, 2020).

2   As quoted at Zack O'Malley Greenburg, "The Easiest Way to Save $1000 on Your Taxes," *Forbes*, August 9, 2011, https://www.forbes.com/sites/moneybuilder/2010/12/23/the-easiest-way-to-save-money-on-your-taxes/.

3   Helvering v. Gregory, 69 F. 2d 809 (2d Cir. 1934), Justia, https://law.justia.com/cases/federal/appellate-courts/F2/69/809/1562063/.

4   Raymond C. Odom, "The 'Goal Standard' of Estate Planning," Northern Trust, updated May 2020, https://cdn.northerntrust.com/pws/documents/white-papers/wealth-management/the-goal-standard-of-estate-planning.pdf.

Chapter 9

1   For example, Russ Alan Prince and Hannah Shaw Grove, *Inside the Family Office: Managing the Fortunes of the Exceptionally Wealthy* (Wealth Management Press, 2004).

2   Adapted from James E. Hughes Jr., *Family Wealth—Keeping It in the Family: How Family Members and Their Advisers Preserve Human, Intellectual, and Financial Assets for Generations*, rev. ed. (Bloomberg Press, 2004).

Chapter 10

1   A.R. Ammons, "A Poem Is a Walk," *Epoch*, Fall 1968.

Also by the Author

The Widow's Bridge: The Surviving Spouse's Guide
to Emotional and Financial Well-being
(2004)

The Coming Widow Boom: What You and Your Loved Ones
Can Do to Prepare for the Unthinkable
(2007)

Ridiculously Rich or Truly Wealthy?
It's more than just money.
(2015)

Family Fiduciary Secrets Video Series
(2024)